GUIDES TO ASSESSMENT IN EDUCATION

General Editor: Jack Wrigley

Assessment

FROM PRINCIPLES TO ACTION

Assessment
FROM PRINCIPLES TO ACTION

Edited by

Robin Lloyd-Jones
Elizabeth Bray
George Johnson
Ruth Currie

GUIDES TO ASSESSMENT IN EDUCATION
General Editor: Jack Wrigley

MACMILLAN

First published 1986
Reprinted 1986

Published by
MACMILLAN EDUCATION LTD
Houndmills, Basingstoke, Hampshire RG21 2XS
and London
Companies and representatives
throughout the world

Printed in Hong Kong

British Library Cataloguing in Publication Data
Lloyd-Jones, Robin
Assessment : from principles to action.—
(Guides to assessment in education)
1. Grading and marking (Students) 2. Education,
Secondary—Great Britain
I. Title II. Bray, Elizabeth III. Series
373.12'64   LB3056.G7
ISBN 0 – 333 – 38620 – 5
ISBN 0-333-38621-3 Pbk

Contents

PART III   SOME ASSESSMENT TECHNIQUES

8 Examinations in Schools RUTH CURRIE   119

9 Profiling ELIZABETH BRAY   141

Introduction

This book is a response to a plea for help from many classroom teachers who do not feel sufficiently familiar with the wide range of new approaches to assessment which they may well be called upon to implement.

Teachers are at the very centre of these changes. More than anyone else, they are the ones who will be expected to 'flesh out' proposals and guidelines and give them a workable form. This innovative role is making and will continue to make fresh demands upon the professional skills of teachers. *Assessment: From Principles to Action* seeks to support teachers both in their desire to acquire new skills and techniques and in their quest to improve upon a vital aspect of education.

In England and Wales the 1981 circular *Curriculum 11-16: Working Papers by H. M. Inspectorate* asking LEA s and schools to review their curricular policies, was followed by a second circular in 1983 asking for a progress report. Both of these had far-reaching implications for assessment, as did Sir Keith Joseph's Sheffield speech early in 1984, which outlined proposals for an examination system that would pay greater attention to the needs of the bottom 40 per cent of pupils and would measure pupils against set levels of achievement. In Scotland, the Munn and Dunning reports have resulted in the phased introduction of the new 14-16 Standard Grade Examination based upon grade-related criteria. *Assessment: From Principles to Action* takes account of the many proposals and reports which will influence the future shape of assessment, but it is more than a review of government initiatives. It aims to explain, in jargon-free language, the basic elements and principles behind these new approaches and to set them in their wider context. It tries, also, to recognise the realities of the classroom and to look closely at the ways in which new modes and techniques of assessment are being used and to provide examples of them in action.

Teachers were expressing dissatisfaction with existing assessment practices well before the publication of the documents mentioned. Nine years ago, as Director of Dunbartonshire's Curriculum Development Centre, I conducted a survey of what teachers felt to be their most pressing in-service training needs. Overwhelmingly the plea was for help with new approaches to assessment. The starting-point for this book was the material devised in response to this expressed need, materials which were shaped and modified by several years of use in workshop sessions, school-based discussions groups and experimental projects. When, in 1981, I moved to another post, much of this material became outdated. However, such was the volume of enquiry from all over the United Kingdom about its availability, that we decided to write an entirely new book, updating and extending the information and taking a fresh and more comprehensive look at the underlying issues – a book which we hope you will find useful.

I would like to thank all the people, too numerous to name individually, who have helped in one way or another in bringing this book into existence. In particular, I would like to acknowledge the contributions of: the former members of our Curriculum Development Centre; the subject advisers of what, before regionalisation, used to be Dunbartonshire; the many teachers in the area who used the initial materials and made valuable comments; the many institutions from which working examples have been taken; and the numerous authors whom we have quoted. Above all, I owe thanks to my co-editor, Elizabeth Bray, who is largely responsible for the final shape of the book and to the other two co-authors, Ruth Currie and George Johnson, whose contributions to the thinking and planning behind the book went well beyond the chapters attributed to them.

Robin Lloyd-Jones

1

An Overview of Assessment

Assessment lies at the core of learning. It is also a major current issue, and an area where rapid changes are taking place. This book offers a bridge between current practice and the changes which are being introduced into assessment. It seeks to build on sound practice and experience, combining these with newer approaches which have proved effective and stimulating to good learning. We have written firstly for classroom teachers – teachers seeking to improve their own assessment practices and to adapt to changing demands – but many of the issues raised are highly relevant for working parties within schools who are hammering out their school's response to the new forms of assessment being introduced into the examination system.

Before we go any further we need to be clear in our own minds what is meant by assessment in education. What are the differences between evaluation, assessment, testing and examinations?

The broadest of these terms is evaluation. Evaluation includes the process of identifying what are the actual educational outcomes, and comparing them with the anticipated outcomes, but goes beyond this. For evaluation involves judgements about the nature, value and desirability of educational outcomes.

Assessment is an all-embracing term. It covers any of the situations in which some aspect of a pupil's education is, in some sense, measured, whether this measurement is by a teacher, an examiner or indeed the pupil himself or herself. Broadly speaking, assessment is concerned with how well the pupil has done, evaluation with whether it was worth doing in the first place. Evaluation cannot take place without assessment; and assessment which is completely divorced from evaluation is a half-measure.

Assessment is often equated with tests and examinations. This is misleading, since neither are essential to assessment. A test is a particular situation set up for the purpose of making an assessment, while an examination is just a large-scale test, or a combination of several tests and other assessment procedures. There are, as we shall see, many other approaches to assessment.

Why Assess?

Why assess? What are the main purposes of assessment? What should be assessed? What should be the scope of assessment? Who is to be assessed, and when, and by whom? How should we assess?

Unless we are clear about why we are assessing, we are unlikely to make the right decisions about when, and what, and how, and by whom.

Formative or Summative?

One fundamental decision we need to make is whether the assessment is formative or summative.

With formative assessment, assessment is integral with the learning, and takes place throughout learning. Assessment gives the teacher and the learner feedback, information about whether the learning objectives are being reached. It provides information on areas of weakness, and also on strengths and potential. For pupils, it is a form of attention and encouragement, and an important ingredient of motivation. The more immediate the feedback, the more useful the information.

The teacher too needs constant feedback on whether the teaching/learning objectives are being achieved. Much of his or her day-to-day teaching strategy will depend on this information.

Summative assessment, however, is concerned with the final summing up. The judgements it makes are for the benefit of people other than the learner. Usually the concern is to differentiate between pupils, so that selection can be made. This type of assessment often comes at the end of a course, or a school career. The difference, however, lies less in the timing than in the intentions of the assessor.

Summative assessment is strongly established in most schools. It is entrenched in the public examination system. Great importance is attached to it by parents, employers and the public in general. There is a real danger than the assessment tail may wag the curriculum dog: that summative assessments, particularly external examinations, may determine rather than reflect the nature and methodology of the curriculum.

Comparisons and Standards

Assessment is undertaken because we are interested in outcomes and in standards. This depends on making comparisons. The performance of pupils may be compared with that of other members of their class, or of their year, or with what are understood to be the norms of performance for (say) all 16-year-olds. This is known as norm-referenced assessment. Alternatively, the comparison may be with the pupil's previous standard of performance. Many of the comments on behaviour in school reports, for example, are 'self-referenced' (sometimes known as ipsitive referencing). Increasingly common is comparison between the pupil's performance and standards set (criteria) for the achievement of learning objectives. This is known as criterion-referenced assessment.

Information for Decision-making

Too often a great deal of time and effort goes into devising, administering and marking pupils' work, tests and examinations, but little attention is paid to presenting the assessment in a way which makes a full interpretation and effective action possible.

Assessment provides the information upon which many decisions are based. These decisions include pupils' decisions (affecting their attitude to their work, and personal, curricular and vocational choices); teachers' decisions about methods, materials and approaches; and school decisions about organisation, curriculum and guidance (see Figure 1.1).

Assessment, however, has far-reaching effects. For individuals, assessments, particularly public examinations, profoundly affect life chances, not just in the first years after leaving school, but ten, twenty or even forty years later.

The public looks to assessment to provide information of various kinds. Public examinations provide ranking and selection criteria for employers, for higher and further education and, in the eyes of the community, provides validation of the education system and generally recognised qualifications. A school's success in the assessment stakes may also influence prospective parents.

Various assessment procedures – HMI reports, standardised tests, administered nationally and regionally – are used by official bodies to monitor standards or evaluate the effectiveness of some particular method or policy. Indeed, the effectiveness of the curriculum as a whole needs to be constantly monitored in the interests of public accountability and to provide information for educational planning and policy-making. Assess-

Decisions by	Affecting	What assessment can contribute
Pupils	Effort, concentration	Motivation. (N.B. fear of failure is often the driving force in competitive assessment. Constant failure is a powerful disincentive)
	Learning skills	Understanding of own strengths and weaknesses
	Curricular choices	Self-knowledge, understanding of level of achievement, interests and potential
	Vocational choices	As above, but also including work-related attitudes and characteristics
Parents	Parental support	Information, improved communication between home, child and school
Teachers	Teaching methods and materials	Information relevant to grouping so that pupils can work at their own pace and level (streaming, setting, grouping within the class, individualised work schemes, etc.)
		Improvement of methods and materials (pupils' poor performance may be due to ineffective teaching)
	Diagnosis for remediation and development	Insight into individual pupils' learning problems and weaknesses
		Insight into pupils' strengths and potential
	Pastoral care	Insight into pubils' abilities, potential, problems, etc.
Schools	School organisation	Setting, streaming. Curricular decisions. Setting up course options. Timetabling, etc.
	School policy	Evaluation.

Figure 1.1   Assessment and decisions within school

ment provides an index to current performance, and is an area of concern to recent governments striving to 'improve' standards.

Assessment within the Context of Educational Aims and Philosophy

In the past thirty years there have been a number of recognisable trends which have profoundly affected the way we view the assessment process:

* Classes were once treated as homogeneous units; recently there has appeared an increasing recognition of individual differences.
* The old emphasis on content is being balanced by a new emphasis on the learning process and on concepts and skills.
* The 'two-by-four' dimensions of learning (two covers of a textbook and four walls of a classroom) are giving way to multi-media materials, practical and oral work, links with the community and so on.
* There is less emphasis on factual knowledge and academic studies and more on social, emotional, moral and aesthetic development.
* The main role of schools was that of the transmitters of past culture; nowadays they are also expected to participate in the transformation of present and future society.
* Individual competition between pupils is being supplemented by new strategies for collaborative working.

By far the most profound change, however, has been a major shift in priorities. The major preoccupation, the main activity which won the school prestige, used in many cases to be the selection and intensive academic tutoring of a small but highly important minority to get them through competitive public examinations and into higher education. For the rest, the majority of the school population, employment lay ahead – and, provided they could read and write and do arithmetic, that was that. The emphasis has changed. The gifted minority is still important, but schools are focusing too on the needs of the majority. There are considerable pressures for a raising of standards of performance of all young people, judged not through competitive examinations (designed to select the ablest), but against descriptions of performance (criteria). Schools are being asked to see education as a preparation for life: there is a new stress on literacy and numeracy, on core subjects, on vocational training, on lifelong skills, and survival skills for unemployment.

These trends influence the answers currently being found to the key questions in assessment – Why assess? What are the main purposes of assessment? What should be assessed? What should be the scope of assessment? Who is to be assessed?, and When and by whom?

In the last decade, in particular, there has been renewed debate about pupils' assessment which is now beginning to affect not merely the terminal examinations taken by pupils at the ages of 16, 17 or 18, but also all assessment which occurs in schools – the subject of this book. Some of these trends are summarised in Figure 1.2.

Trend away from	Trend towards
Summative assessment in a formal setting (exams)	Formative and informal assessments
Examinations on infrequent and special occasions	Continuous assessment, often as a normal part of the teaching/learning process
Comparing pupils with each other, to indicate final achievement and for ranking and selection purposes	Comparing pupils' performance with predetermined criteria, to provide feedback for improving performance
External responsibility for setting and marking examinations	Internal responsibility for assessment; professionalism of teachers acknowledged; self-assessment by pupils
Recall of course content	Stress on learning process, e.g. information retrieval, study skills
Assessment concerned with academic achievement, with content, within established subjects	Recognition given to skills such as listening, speaking, practical skills, attitudes, personal and social development
Assessment in artificial situations (exam halls) and dominated by the concern to be cheatproof	Assessment in situations more akin to real life, e.g. practical projects, folio assessment, 'open book' examinations
Assessment as a self-contained activity	More awareness of education as a continuum and that curriculum and assessment should take account of what comes before and follows after. Assessment seen as an integral part of the curriculum and of teaching/learning

Figure 1.2   Trends in assessment

Assessment: From Principles to Action

Many of these trends are assisted by new technology and the increasing use of computer-assisted assessment will accelerate change and open up new possibilities.

Remember, these are only trends. Some teachers and some schools might recognise themselves more by the traditional forms of assessment (left-hand column). Others are already much influenced by the newer trends. Most schools are probably a mixture of both or half-way between the two.

The Need for a Whole-school Policy

There is a strong case for all schools having a clear assessment policy which provides coherence to the activities of different departments and individual teachers. Coherence, rather than uniformity, is the key.

Assessment is closely connected with the school's whole-value system. Diverging policies within a school are confusing to pupils, parents and teachers. Too many different styles of reporting is less helpful to parents in obtaining an overview of their child's progress than a unified system would be. Pupils, in particular, need to feel that their school has agreed aims and priorities, that there is a common ethos and that everyone is pulling in the same direction on their behalf.

Coherence means that more effective use can be made in school of the information gathered through assessment. Unless the aims of those who conduct the assessment and those who make use of the information in school are shared, there will be instances of useful information being unrecorded, not put to use, or not followed up, and there will be other instances of important information which is required but is not forthcoming. Without some common system of assessment and recording, overall patterns of weakness and strength in a pupil may go unobserved: impending problems will be overlooked, potential missed.

Moreover, without a coherent assessment system, evaluation of the school's aims and objectives – of curricular outcomes – is extremely difficult.

Obviously a school's assessment policy will be influenced by such factors as whether the school tends to be 'community-centred', 'child-centred' or 'subject-centred'; by the relative emphasis on the social, moral, emotional and academic development of the child; by the extent to which external examinations dominate the curriculum and learning styles of all pupils.

The reality of the situation is that, within any one school, individual teachers will have differing views about the aims and methods of assessment; they will be in differing states of readiness for change, both in terms of their attitudes to innovation and in terms of their technical and professional competence to put new methods into practice.

Probably the greatest challenge to policy-makers in schools is to achieve coherent whole-school policies while maintaining flexibility; to cater for differing needs of different subjects, differing classes and differing age groups and ability levels, while avoiding fragmentation. One of the characteristics of successful policy-making is the extent to which members of staff have been involved, through consultation, working parties, in-service training and professional support from colleagues. If this book assists in this process, it will have served its purpose.

The last years of this century are likely to be periods of immense change. Some changes will arise from external pressures – pressures from government, further and higher education, employers. Some will be the result of changes in our society, our culture, our priorities as a community. In addition, changes based on information technology will radically affect all recording and communication in schools (and these lie at the core of the assessment process).

Both primary and secondary schools will be under continuing pressures to make changes in curricular and assessment practices. Individual teachers, while they can improve their assessment practices, cannot usually make major changes in isolation. Successful innovation occurs within the context of agreed departmental and whole-school policy.

A coherent policy, based on agreed guidelines, is far more robust, flexible, supportive and open to innovation than a system based on past practice and individual preferences.

The Plan of the Book

Part I: Key Concepts in Assessment

First, we consider **fitness for purpose**. Here the concept of 'fitness for purpose' is explored in relation to the choices we can make: choices of modes (and techniques), choice of media and choice of frame of reference.

By 'mode' is meant the general nature, style and character of the assessment, and thus (by implication) its values, emphases and intentions. For example, an external examination is a different mode from continuous assessment. Techniques, however, are the instruments, methods or tools employed – for example, objective tests, essays and so on. The techniques are discussed in greater detail later.

The choice of media (the form, for example the medium of writing or the medium of the spoken word) is then considered both in relation to the evidence (pupils' performance) on which we make the assessment, and in relation to how we respond (do we respond in writing or orally?)

Finally, this chapter considers the choice of 'frames of references' - the choice between norm-referenced assessment and criterion-referenced assessment.

Next we consider **validity and reliability** (Chapter 3).

No one can claim that his assessment has perfect validity (that it does exactly what it is meant to do) or perfect reliability (that the assessment is absolutely consistent, and that the variables have been reduced to zero). It is foolish and dangerous to attach great significance to the fact that one student gets 52 per cent and his or her neighbour 48 per cent.

So validity is one of the key issues in assessment. Are we indeed testing what we think we are testing? Have we really obtained the information we were seeking? Can we be satisfied with the objectivity and consistency of our assessment? Have factors like handwriting or the dress and speech of the pupil influenced our judgement at an unconscious level? Questions such as these are explored in Chapter 3, although they recur throughout the book.

Part II: Some Assessment Techniques

Next we turn to a detailed consideration of some assessment techniques (Chapter 4, 5 and 6).

These techniques include **objective tests** (Chapter 4), **structured questions and essays** (Chapter 5) and **extended assignments and projects** (Chapter 6). In theory, at one extreme of the continuum, the assessment system is almost totally closed, and at the other end the assessment system is almost totally open-ended (Figure 1.3).

Most books about assessment have been concerned with formal tests and examinations, and display a preoccupation with measurement. They have concentrated on the closed end of the assessment spectrum, and paid relatively little attention to the open end. They are also more concerned with the public uses of assessment than the private uses (Figure 1.4). In practice a great deal of assessment is obtained informally, without tests, for example, through observing the pupil, through informal conversations, unrecorded classroom questioning. And much of the value of assessment lies in its private uses. Such activities help build up a more complete picture of the pupil and his or her capabilities, with constant feedback to both pupil and teacher. However, the dangers of relying too heavily on

Closed system	Open-ended system
Pupil selects answer from given alternatives	Content, structure and style of answer determined by the pupil
Only one correct answer is possible	Answer is a matter of opinion and judgement
Pupils' answers easily compared	Pupils' answers differ widely, comparability low
Extensive, superficial sampling of course content	Limited, in-depth, assessment of course objectives

Continuum between closed and open-ended systems: examples:

Objective tests	Structured questions	Guided questions	Open-ended essays	Self-selected projects

Figure 1.3   Closed and open-ended assessment

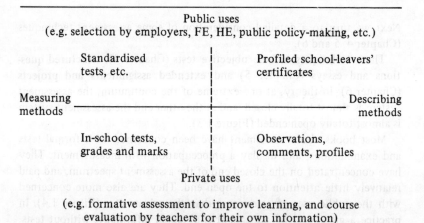

Public uses
(e.g. selection by employers, FE, HE, public policy-making, etc.)

Measuring methods	Standardised tests, etc.	Profiled school-leavers' certificates	Describing methods
	In-school tests, grades and marks	Observations, comments, profiles	

Private uses

(e.g. formative assessment to improve learning, and course evaluation by teachers for their own information)

Figure 1.4   Assessment dimensions: public and private uses; methods based on measurement and description

what could be little more than subjective and untested impressions, should also be borne in mind.

Part III: Assessment Strategies

The choice between **norm- and criterion-referenced assessment** is discussed in detail in Chapter 7. Should we base our assessment strategy on a familiar norm-referenced framework? That is, should the basis for comparison be between pupils, with the object of assessment being to produce a rank order based on 'norms' or how far each pupil is from the average? Or should we base our assessment strategy on criteria – that is, on statements about learning objectives, so that the pupil's success is measured by how far she/he succeeds in mastering the learning objectives specified in the criteria?

We then turn, in Chapters 8 and 9, to a consideration of two assessment strategies that may complement each other or may be alternatives: the **traditional examination** (Chapter 8) and the newer **profile** (Chapter 9). Profiles are detailed, comprehensive statements, usually systematic and open, about a pupil's achievements. They may include examinations results but go beyond these to assess competencies and capabilities, skills, learning experiences and aptitudes and attitudes. Profiles tend to be linked with continuous assessment, and can be used both formatively and summatively.

The weight attached to examinations as an assessment strategy will depend to an important extent on your philosophy of education. The decision to adopt profiling will also depend on whether you believe that the profile offers a more valid and reliable method of assessing learning outcomes which you see as educational, but non-examinable, objectives.

We need to use assessment information positively and to communicate it in a helpful way to students and parents. In order to do this, ways have to be found of overcoming the 'inscrutability' of marks and grades. The wider the span of activities and skills reported in a single grade, the less useful it is. Unless supported by other information or comment, a single grade or mark could be inscrutable to the point of becoming almost meaningless to the recipients of the information.

The last chapter deals therefore with **Reports** (Chapter 10) and is particularly concerned with how we can move away from the 'basic information' model of reports to parents to an 'involvement' model, which uses assessment information as the basis for discovering the pupil's potential, his or her strengths and learning problems, aptitudes and interests, and from there to move forward to a plan to improve learning.

Some of the Main Themes of this Book

Certain issues emerge again and again throughout the next nine chapters:

The basic aim of assessment is to promote pupils' learning. Assessment can only be justified if it benefits, either directly or indirectly, our children's learning. It is not an end in itself. These are dangers in over-assessment and assessment should always have a clear purpose.

We need to be clear about aims and objectives. We must be clear about exactly what we intend to assess; about what the objectives of our teaching are; and which learning outcomes we wish to assess, and for what purpose.

Fitness for purpose is the key. The methods of assessment chosen should be appropriate to the reason for the assessment and the type of information being sought. It should be relevant to the skill or content area being assessed and to the nature of the subject.

In practice the choice of technique is often best approached by eliminating the obviously inappropriate techniques. For example, a written test for a practical skill which has been learnt through practical methods is inappropriate.

Validity and reliability are key considerations. We should be guided in our choice of technique by the intended learning outcomes and the need for an assessment which is reliable and consistent. It is not only a matter of what we want to assess, but also of what actually is being assessed.

Lastly, **assessment is not just something tacked on to the end of a course or unit.** It is part of the learning process and must be planned as such. This means that if you make changes in assessment methodology it will have curriculum repercussions – for example, on timetabling, resources, lesson-planning and teaching methods. Similarly, if you change curricular objectives or methods, you will need to change your assessment.

The Limitation of Assessment

There are many excellent reasons for assessment. It is, as I have argued, an integral part of the learning experience. It is an indispensable tool for the teacher. But I would like to end this chapter with a reminder. The tools of assessment are crude and imperfect, and they often deal with factors that are intangible and very difficult to measure.

There is much research and field work still to be done. We can hope to narrow, but probably never completely close, the gap between what we, as teachers, would like to assess and the techniques available to assess them effectively. At present, we are only assessing a small fraction of what our students learn, and there is always the danger of emphasising one aspect because it is assessable and neglecting another because it is not. Aims not reflected in assessment procedures do not achieve the same status as those which are.

Perhaps all assessment should be accompanied by a warning notice similar to that issued by a Sussex University Working Party on B. A. Degree Assessment:

> Prospective employers should be warned that the usefulness of the result is limited. First, because the predictive value of a particular class of degree cannot be guaranteed; second, because the actual measurement is extremely rough; third, because the classified degree may be measuring qualities which are not necessarily relevant to the purposes an employer may have in mind.

This book as a whole contains no instant solutions. It cannot offer the final word. It does, however, suggest new approaches and give solid examples of them. But there are no easy alternatives. Most require a great deal of hard work and preparation to implement, although they are also productive and rewarding.

Education must respond to the changing needs of society, to new branches of knowledge, to changing perceptions of its role and to refinements in its techniques. Assessment, in particular, is a developing area of of education with much field work and research still to be done, both by teachers within schools and by educationalists. Rapid developments in assessment will test and challenge the professionalism, experience and expertise of teachers and schools, and their ability to respond positively and creatively. If this book contributes to this, and hastens its own obsolescence, it will have succeeded.

PART I

KEY CONCEPTS IN ASSESSMENT

2
Fitness for Purpose

Fitness for purpose is a key concept in assessment. Very early in planning an assessment strategy you are faced with certain questions. What are your course objectives? What learning outcomes are you seeking? How will you assess your pupils' progress towards these outcomes?

Without assessment you and your pupils will never know how far you – and they – have achieved the course objectives. Yet the assessment process will also shape – perhaps distort – your curricular objectives.

In this chapter I concentrate on some key concepts that relate to fitness of purpose.

First of all we consider the choice of modes (I will explain this term in a moment) and the relationship between modes and techniques. Next we look at the choices of media (the form, such as the medium of writing or the medium of the spoken work) both in relation to the evidence (pupil performances) on which we make assessments, and in relation to how we respond (for example, do we respond in writing, or orally?) Finally we look at the choice of frames of references – should the assessment be norm-referenced or criterion-referenced? (Again these terms will be explained.)

Assessment is multi-dimensional, and the concepts outlined above are in a sense possible dimensions. If we fail to realise the various dimensions we are unlikely to choose the assessment which best fits our purposes.

Modes and Techniques

By 'mode' I mean the general nature, style and character of the assessment and (by implication) its values, emphases and intentions. Thus 'mode' is the overall form of the assessment, whereas the 'technique' of assessment is, more narrowly, the methods, tools or instruments employed in the assessment, whatever the mode. An analogy may help to clarify the distinction. Painters use certain techniques, tools and materials - brushes, paints,charcoal, pen and ink and so on - but may be working in entirely different genre or 'modes': portrait painting, abstracts, landscape, still life. So too a teacher or assessor may use similar techniques or tools - multi-choice questions or essay questions, for example - within quite different 'modes'. You may, for example, decide on continuous assessment as the mode best suited to one course, while preferring an end-of-term examination mode for another course. In both you may use similar techniques - for example, a comprehension exercise - but when and why you use this technique, how you use it and what you do with the results may be fundamentally different.

A Choice of Modes

The techniques of assessment are listed in Figure 2.1. The choice of techniques is wide, and will be the subject of detailed discussion in Chapters 4, 5 and 6.

In this chapter I propose to begin by opening up the discussion about modes of assessment. If you are only using one or two modes you may well be failing to meet some of your curricular objectives, and it is worth considering whether a different or additional approach - a different mode - may in fact be useful.

Our choice of modes determines many aspects of assessment. First, it determines when the assessment takes place: at the end of a term or throughout the course? The mode will depend on who is the assessor - the teacher or an external examiner? The mode depends, too, on assumptions about who should be the main beneficiary: is the assessment mainly to help the pupil with his learning or to decide who is to get a place at university, a job or entry to an 'O' level course? Is the assessment to help you evaluate your teaching or to demonstrate to the public, parents, employers or HMIs that the school is doing a good job? The choice of mode will decide how we assess, what we assess and what we do with the assessments. Behind these choices is the most important question of all - why we assess.

The assumptions behind some traditional choices of modes (for example, formal written examinations for most, but not all, pupils at 16+) are being questioned by much recent public discussion. It is not simply that dissatisfaction is felt about some of the techniques employed, though these are questioned. For example, doubts are expressed about whether multi-choice questions do not trivialise learning, and whether essays in examinations can fairly sample a two-year course. But more fundamentally the whole character and values – the mode – of the assessment is being re-examined.

Different modes of assessment do not fit into easily labelled compartments, just as few teaching styles can be immediately classified. At best we can identify certain tendencies or characteristics which differentiate one style from another, and add up to a difference of mode. Many of the modes mentioned below do, in fact, overlap or merge with each other.

Some modes, particularly the more traditional, you will recognise immediately. Others may be unfamiliar. No one mode is 'best' for all situations.

I have paired and contrasted modes to emphasise the differences in approach. In many instances both of the contrasting modes may be appropriate at different times in a course you are teaching, for different purposes. Your choice of mode will depend on fitness for purpose. This includes the nature of the subject, the aims and objectives of the course, the purpose for which the assessment information is required, the needs of your students, and, of course, your own personal teaching style.

Here, then, are some of the questions a practising teacher might ask of himself or herself about the choice of modes:

Formal or Informal?

Should the mode of assessment be formal or informal?

The most formal assessment mode is the public examination. School examinations, and tests, are also deliberately contrived situations, as are auditions for orchestras, or job interviews.

Informal assessment takes place inevitably most of the time: we are continually summing one another up. Much of a teacher's interaction with his or her pupils is informal assessment – a word of praise or sarcasm, a smile or a rebuke, convey a valuation of the pupil or his or her work.

We can also use planned but informal assessment as part of an assessment strategy. For example, your recorded observations may be a much more valid assessment than a formal examination when you are assessing a pupil's ability to make a weld, to respond to music through dance, to converse in French or use a reference library.

Final or Continuous?

Should we concentrate on an assessment which is final or a procedure which is concurrent with the course ('continuous assessment')?

Table 2.1 Some Assessment Techniques

Discussed chapter(s)	Techniques	Description	Advantages	Problems
4	Objective tests (i.e. objective, not subjective)	Single word/phrase answer; multi-choice questions; Cloze procedure. Used in computer-assisted learning	An efficient means of sampling recall of curriculum widely if superficially. Useful in diagnostic assessment. Very quick and easy to mark. Objective	Over-use makes learning routine; trivialises response. Not valid if poorly designed. Poor at assessing higher cognitive (thinking) skills. Useless for assessing creativity, etc.
5	Structured questions	Stem + sub-questions. Used in worksheets to structure and sequence learning, as well as in tests	Good at sampling recall. Very useful in diagnostic assessment. Easy and quick to mark. Objective	Over-use makes learning routine and trivial. Usually poor at assessing higher cognitive (thinking) skills, creativity, etc.
4, 5	Comprehension exercises	Stem + sub-questions. Stem may be a poem, extract from book or article, maps, historical documents, etc.	If well constructed, good at assessing ability to make inferences. Fairly easy to mark, fairly objective	Over-use makes learning trivial and routine. Badly designed test is demotivating and damaging. Little scope for creativity
5	Extended writing	Essays (guided or open-ended) also journal-writing, field work reports, creative writing, etc.	Enables pupil to structure own writing developing thinking, writing and study skills. Opportunities for formative assessment	Time-consuming and difficult, especially for poor writers. Difficult to mark objectively. Poor at sampling coverage of curriculum

6	Projects: written/practical	Field work (e.g. Geography) investigation (e.g. History). Projects in technical subjects, computer studies, home economics, etc.	Opportunity to develop thinking, communication, and information, retrieval, aesthetic appreciation, and practical and psycho-motor skills	Time-consuming. Objectives/criteria must be clear. Assessment somewhat subjective
8	Open-book examinations/Tests	Exam technique in which student has access to reference materials, text of play, own notes, etc.	Tests access skills (i.e. information retrieval), so resembles adult situations	Not traditional. Objectives/criteria must be carefully designed, and students trained
7, 9	Profiles Observations	Checklist of criteria to describe attainments or description of behaviours, personal qualities, etc.	Can be used to monitor pupil's progress and attainments using criteria (objectives). Can be used to check basic skills (writing, number) and social and life skills (perseverence, co-operation, etc.)	May be highly subjective and judgemental in assessing personal qualities. Poorly designed descriptors may be irrelevant or distorting

Final assessment (or terminal assessment) occurs, obviously, at the end of a course. Examples include the old 11+, end-of-term examinations, 'O' and 'A' levels and CSE, university finals, and driving tests. In most (but not all) cases the final examination will be of the curriculum taught.

In contrast, continuous assessment takes place throughout the course. 'Continuous' is, perhaps, a misnomer. It is impossible to assess all pupils all the time. Such assessment usually takes place at regular intervals throughout the course. There are complex but important arguments both for and against each mode.

Formative or Summative?

Formative assessment is assessment primarily designed to help the pupil progress. It is supportive of learning: it may be non-judgemental and concentrate on positive encouragement and constructive criticism. Formative assessment is thus often informal. Summative assessment is concerned with a final summing up, and is often used for grading, ranking and selection purposes. 'O' and 'A' levels are summative.

Internal or External?

Should the assessment be for, or by, internal assessors or external assessors?

This is an area in which most individual teachers do not have much choice. External assessment is the norm in public examinations. These are set and marked by external agents (examination boards), and are mainly intended for external users: university selectors, employers and, in a more general sense, the public and their elected representatives in local and central government. External examinations are seen as validating courses, and their influence on the curriculum is profound.

To a limited extent public examinations also use teachers as assessors. A few teachers have, of course, long been involved as paid employees of examination boards in setting examinations. Many more mark examination papers, but they do not mark their own pupils' work. In CSE Mode III, and in the Foundation levels of the new Scottish certificates, teachers are intimately involved in constructing the curriculum and assessing their pupils, often with some external moderation to validate both courses and assessment procedures.

Internal assessment and internal syllabuses do not necessarily go together. It is possible to assess performance in external syllabus by internal means. For example, project work in a technology course or computer studies, or field work in Geography, may be internally assessed. Similarly, an internal syllabus may be assessed by a local consortium of teachers working on an agreed marking scheme, which, in principle, is a form of external assessment.

Internal assessment of an internally devised syllabus brings greater freedom of choice and opportunities to do such things as field work, projects, simulations, drama and practical work. It allows teachers to use their intimate and detailed knowledge of the work of individual pupils across a wide range of activities and objectives, over a long period of time. There are dangers, not least that teacher's judgements may be subjective, or lack standardisation. The new freedom imposes new disciplines on a teacher and demands familiarity with new assessment techniques.

Internal assessment may be conducted for in-school purposes – for example, to decide who follows which course, or it may be mainly for the information of the teacher and his pupils. It is even possible to completely internalise assessment: a pupil's self-assessment may be a purely private affair, or may be fostered in a non-judgemental way by a teacher, solely for the benefit of the pupil.

Process or Product?

Should the assessment mode concentrate on the process or the product?

The end-product may only reflect a small part of the process. For example, it may not be possible from looking at, and even tasting, a cake, to assess how far the pupil has acquired the ability to use recipe books, budget, plan his use of time and master various techniques. Both the 'knowledge explosion' with its vast increase in the amount of facts available to us all, and the pace of change in our society which demands flexibility of thought and ability to handle new information and new situations, have placed much greater emphasis on the learning process.

Convergent or Divergent?

In some forms of assessment there is only one correct answer. Multi-choice questions, and all objective tests, are based on convergent answers. Recordings of teachers in classwork show that often teachers expect only convergent answers: they ask questions to which they already know the answer, and reject any diversions, even if, in fact, the pupil supplies new and relevant information, or a correct but alternative answer.

Divergent answers are much less easy to mark than convergent. How do you assess creativity, or imagination, or problem-formulation and -solving in situations where there is no unique correct solution? Yet many would argue that these are far more important curricular objectives than correct recall of given information.

Assessment procedures based solely on convergence not divergence have profound and not always beneficial effects on the curriculum.

Competitive or Non-Competitive?

Traditionally, most assessment in secondary schools has been competitive. Supporters of competitive examinations would say that competition is a fact of life. Grading is necessary to enable selection to take place for further education and the job markets. Success (or failure) in competitive examination provides pupils and parents with vital information for making curricular and career decisions. Moreover that pupils, parents, employers and the public expect competitive examinations. Finally it is seen as a motivator.

The school system has been largely based on competition: it is inherent in all decisions about placing pupils (streaming). Pupils are well aware, even in primary school that the 'red' table seats the best readers. In secondary schools the youngsters who fail in the system are all too aware that they are 'thick'. The beneficiaries of this system are institutions – universities, employers – who are able to cream off the most successful pupils.

While many successful children are strongly motivated by competition it is doubtful whether it has anything but a demotivating effect on the less able. There are, however, non-competitive forms of assessment. The achievement of pupils can, for example, be measured against course objectives (criteria). Here the aim of the course is to ensure that all pupils achieve the objectives (mastery learning), though scope is often allowed for quick workers to extend their learning in projects.

Self-assessment can also be non-competitive.

Summary: Modes and Techniques

Many teachers are not fully conscious of the range of assessment possibilities. Yet they are uneasily aware that not all their pupils are best served by the assessment procedures they are using, and that some curricular objectives cannot be assessed adequately using traditional methods. Current educational thinking is tending to open up the discussion. While not rejecting traditional modes of assessment, new emphases are appearing.

A Choice of Media

Most books on assessment (and this is no exception) tend to concentrate on written performances by children, and written feedback (e.g. numerical grades or marks). Writing and learning are traditionally linked, and assessment based on writing is more highly structured than any other forms of assessment. But it is well to remind ourselves that writing is not the only, nor necessarily the best, medium.

Pupil Performances: A Choice of Media

Figure 2.2 identifies a number of media and shows how these relate to modes:

* *Written forms*

In this we may include not only written forms using language (words), but also all written forms using diagrams, graphs, graphical representations, number, formulae, field-work notes and so on. The advantage of written evidence, apart from the fact that it is traditional, is that is has some sort of permanence; this makes comparisons relatively easy. It is also easily stored, sorted and retrieved. Writing is not always the preferred medium, the form in which assessable pupil performances should be presented. Many pupils have problems with writing and to use only written forms means that they are incapable of performing adequately. Writing is not always appropriate. For example, writing an account of how to bath a baby, or turn a bit of metal on a lathe, is inadequate if we are assessing parenting or engineering, respectively.

* *Practical work*

In practical subjects – anything from technology to home economics, and including art, science practicals, geography field work, business studies, computer studies, drama and so on – we need to distinguish between 'process' and 'product' as 'media'.

Products (sponge cakes, coffee tables, computer programmes) are relatively permanent and fairly easy to assess, but tend to be bulky and/or difficult to store. The process, on the other hand, may be far more important than the product, for the process may involve inquiry skills, identification, diagnosis and solution of problems, implementation of solutions, evaluation of results and so on. However, processes

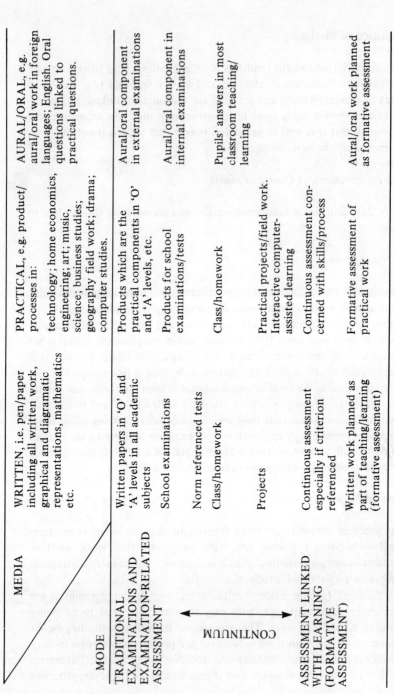

MEDIA / MODE	WRITTEN, i.e. pen/paper including all written work, graphical and diagramatic representations, mathematics etc.	PRACTICAL, e.g. product/processes in: technology; home economics, engineering; art; music, science; business studies; geography field work; drama; computer studies.	AURAL/ORAL, e.g. aural/oral work in foreign languages; English. Oral questions linked to practical questions.
TRADITIONAL EXAMINATIONS AND EXAMINATION-RELATED ASSESSMENT	Written papers in 'O' and 'A' levels in all academic subjects	Products which are the practical components in 'O' and 'A' levels, etc.	Aural/oral component in external examinations
	School examinations	Products for school examinations/tests	Aural/oral component in internal examinations
	Norm referenced tests		
	Class/homework	Class/homework	Pupils' answers in most classroom teaching/learning
	Projects	Practical projects/field work. Interactive computer-assisted learning	
ASSESSMENT LINKED WITH LEARNING (FORMATIVE ASSESSMENT)	Continuous assessment especially if criterion referenced	Continuous assessment concerned with skills/process	
	Written work planned as part of teaching/learning (formative assessment)	Formative assessment of practical work	Aural/oral work planned as formative assessment

CONTINUUM

Note: Pupil behaviours are not included. See text.

Figure 2.2 Medium/mode in which work is presented for assessment

must be assessed as they occur, which makes them more difficult to assess, though the formative assessment of processes is strongly indicated.

* Oral forms

The spoken word, unless recorded, is the least permanent form of evidence, and oral assessment is the least structured. It is therefore often the least discussed in books on assessment although the spoken word is the medium of much classroom learning, and what the pupils say is the basis for much informal assessment (in that we pay attention to, and praise, right answers, and attempt to reject wrong answers, or divergent answers). A new emphasis is appearing on pupils' ability to communicate orally, and this implies assessment.

* Behaviours

Finally, in some senses, pupil performance is also assessed in terms of pupil behaviours, attitudes, responses. In one sense, how we behave (and this may include gestures, facial expressions, body language and many other cues) is one of the most powerful means (media) for communication. Inevitably teachers assess their pupils' behaviour, since how pupils behave is enormously important in the classroom.

The way we assess pupil behaviour can be very important. On the one hand, it is important that we should not allow our personal feelings about pupils to affect other assessment. For example, just because a pupil is attractive and hardworking, he does not necessarily merit a higher mark in mathematics than an unattractive pupil who gets more right answers. This 'halo' effect is particularly dangerous in marking essays. Teachers are human, and they will make (often subconscious) assessments of pupils based on classroom behaviours, personal appearance and attractiveness, and even (to our shame) factors such as sex, social class, accent, race and so on. Unless you recognise your subjective assessment of pupils, and guard against bias, you are unlikely to assess fairly.

This does not mean that we should disregard pupil behaviour for assessment purposes. It is unreal to disregard the 'affective area' (to do with feeling and tone) which is expressed through behaviour (in the broadest sense). Assessment which ignores behaviours is artificial. We also need to be aware that pupils need and deserve assessment in this area. Classroom management is impossible if we do not make assessments (that is, do not respond to or initiate, patterns of behaviour). Second, if we are concerned about the development of pupils, we should regard this development, at least in social and life skills, as a priority area in which we should assess and respond formatively.

Communicating Assessment

But how should we respond? Our response (assessment) can be communicated through a variety of media too. We can communicate our assessments in writing, but we also communicate assessment through various other media. Written forms of assessment are traditional, recognised and recognisable, and can be carefully structured. But written assessment is not necessarily the most potent.

Figure 2.3 is an analysis of the media through which we convey to pupils our assessments of their performances. We may communicate our assessment in written forms, or orally, or through non-verbal means, or through school structures. Most books on assessment concentrate on the assessments in written form (corrections to work, marks, grades, etc., examination results, pupil records and reports to parents). These are clearly important, but written communications, though carefully planned and structured, are relatively infrequent and have less permanence for pupils than is often supposed.

On the other hand, other media for communicating assessment may be more powerful than teachers sometimes assume. Individual teachers can, consciously or subconsciously, transmit powerful messages to pupils about their performance by oral and by non-verbal means. These messages are being transmitted most of the time. This feedback, because it has immediacy and is personal, has probably more effect on pupils' learning than some teachers realise. As every parent knows, children like some teachers and dislike others. Some they fear, others they despise. These attitudes reflect the assessment messages children get from their teachers. By and large, children work hard for teachers they like and respect, and are unco-operative with teachers they dislike. Or, to put it in another way, children respond to assessment messages. The assessment messages you give, consciously or unconsciously, either spoken or (perhaps more influential) in terms of your reactions – your attention, your facial expressions – have a powerful formative influence and this should never be overlooked.

Finally, the whole way the school is run, its structures and methodology, its reward and discipline systems, the curriculum and especially the hidden curriculum, is full of hidden assessment messages for pupils. Much

	Assessment communicated in writing	Assessment communicated orally	Assessment communicated by non-verbal means	Assessment communicated through the school organisation and structure
Public official, visible	Reports in local press of public examinations Public examinations results/certificates School examinations grade/marks/rank order	Public announcement, e.g. examination results/marks read in assembly Prize-day speeches lists of pupils on detention, etc. Parents' evenings	Prize-giving Special privileges Punishments Displays of pupils' work	Selection/rejection of pupils on the basis of assessments or examinations. Placement of pupils in sets, streams, etc. Labelling of pupil groups, e.g. advanced/non-advanced, examination/non certificate
Less public but planned by school or teacher	Testimonials to employers Reports to parents (formal)	Classroom management, e.g. feedback to whole class on homework	Classroom management systems, e.g. seating arrangements	Allocation of resources (staff expertise/time/materials), e.g. giving high timetabling priorities to 'A' level pupils
Intended for individual pupils	Marks/corrections of individual pupils' work. Formative feedback to pupils Formative feedback to parents in detailed reports	Formative feedback to pupils Formative feedback to parents and parents' evenings	Friendly/hostile reaction to pupils	
Subconscious			Approval/disapproval) attention/rejection) expressed non-verbally and unintentionally	Backwash of school assessment system (e.g. competitive examinations shapes curricular and assessment strategies)

Figure 2.3   Form/medium in which assessment is communicated

school organisation is based, after all, on decisions arising from assessment: decisions about setting and streaming, about who will follow advanced courses, who is relegated to remedial departments. Decisions about the allocation of resources are full of assessment messages. Consider the drifting rabble of non-certificate pupils dumped on inexperienced young teachers with few resources, no planned course and poor back-up from senior staff. Both teacher and pupils know all too well that they are the 'thickies'. Often these boys and girls produce so little work (because their writing skills are so poor, and the demands made on them ineffectual) that the only assessment they get is in terms of their status in the school machine. One of the heartening findings of many projects is that well-planned courses, properly resourced, with thorough assessment which is based on achievable learning outcomes (criteria), pays dividends with less able pupils. Assessment is a form of attention, welcome if the assessment is based on what pupils can do rather than what they cannot do.

This brings us to a consideration of the framework of assessment.

A Choice of Frames of Reference

The choice of a frame of reference is crucial if we are considering 'fitness for purpose'. You will almost certainly be aware of the traditional norm-referenced frame which underlies traditional examinations. I will be contrasting this with the more recently introduced criterion-referenced assessment to bring out not only differences between the frames of reference, but the different underlying purposes.

The Purpose of Traditional Examinations

Public examinations - the GCE 'O' and 'A' levels and their predecessors - have exerted an increasing influence on both curriculum and assessment since the public examination was introduced over a century ago. They are widely and favourably regarded as an objective, convenient and credible yardstick of proven worth. They are seen by many as essential to the maintenance of academic standards in schools. They are deeply embedded in the education system, and crucial to the pinnacle of the system - selection for university courses. They exert a profound and (many would argue) beneficial influence on the whole curriculum and on assessment procedures, many of which bolster the effectiveness of 'O' and 'A' levels as a screening and selection device.

Fundamental to the public examination, and to related assessment (the old 11+ competitive examinations in school to determine who is allowed to enter 'O' level courses, and so on), is the concept of 'norms'. Performance is measured against, and relative to, the norms (average level of performance) of others in the 'normative' group: all the other 11 year olds in the county, or all the other third years in a comprehensive school, or all the other 'O' level candidates taking mathematics in that year.

The purpose of assessment within a norm-referenced framework is grading, ranking and comparing. Essentially, a norm-referenced assessment is a screening device. For the pupil, improvement consists in moving up the rank order at the expense of other pupils, or surviving a series of screenings. Pupils who perform badly – and by implication, at least half the pupils will be 'below average' – are 'failures'. Successful pupils proceed to further examinations competing against the new, and higher, norms of the successful group, in which, again, below average pupils (below the average for the new normative group) will fail, and above average will succeed. This (it is argued) provides demanding standards of excellence and successfully motivates the best pupils to strive for the highest levels of achievement.

Since ranking (for selection) is the major concern, examinations must be designed to discriminate between pupils. It is thus unnecessary to sample all the syllabus. It is more important to set questions that will produce a scatter of marks, so that pupils can be ranked.

(a) *IQs of pupils (norm-related test)*

(b) *Scatter of marks produced by well-designed norm-related examination*

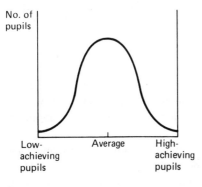

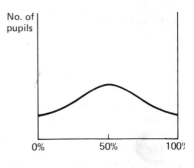

Figure 2.4

A major preoccupation of examiners in a norm-referenced system is to make the examination cheat-proof. Hence the artificial conditions of many examinations: the formal setting, the time limit, the silence, the dependence upon memory rather than the resources (reference books, notes, primary sources, dictionaries, teachers, workmates) which any intelligent adult would use if faced with (for example) a difficult translation from a foreign language, a mathematical problem or the request for an article for a learned journal.

For the pupil the results of norm-referenced tests or examination takes the form of information on how he or she compares with other pupils: a rank order, grade or a single numerical mark. The preoccupation of a norm-referenced system is with the public reporting of performance measured against norms in order that selection can take place, rather than formative feedback for pupils'. Great effort is made to ensure that marking is valid within this constraint, since fairness is an important consideration: examinations affect pupils' life-chances.

The Case against Traditional Examinations

Disquiet has been expressed about examinations. Both employers and universities have serious reservations about the predictive reliability of examinations. Public examinations are used as a screening device for selection by universities, colleges of FE and employers, but there is growing evidence that there is a poor correlation between performance in 'O' and 'A' levels and performance in degree course. Employers report similar findings. Moreover, employers question the relevance of school learning experience. One survey reports that 'the study of craft subjects and particularly those using more innovative methods coincided with higher levels of performance [in work], more so than studying physics in a practical way'.

At the same time, due partly to the raising of the school-leaving age, it has been realised that competitive public examinations have the effect of certifying as 'failures' an alarmingly high proportion of school-leavers. Further, it is argued, norm-related examinations are no way to validate the learning experiences, over the course of eleven years compulsory schooling, of the majority of pupils.

The 'backwash' effect of public examinations, on both curriculum and assessment procedures, has further been questioned as deeper consideration is given to learning objectives. Examinations, it is argued, test mainly trivial and irrelevant learning outcomes and memorisation of factual information. On the whole, they fail to assess what are called 'higher order thinking skills' (comprehension, the ability to apply concepts and understandings, analysis and evaluation) and the 'affective area' (which concerns feelings, tone, empathy and understandings). Examinations are good at assessing the recall of knowledge, but with what has been called the 'knowledge explosion', the recapitulation of second-hand facts is becoming less important. Much more importance is being placed on skills such as information retrieval, on the diagnosis and solution of problems and the implementation of solutions, on the ability to make and take opportunities, to work together co-operatively and to be creative.

Out of this has grown an increasing emphasis on new ways of learning accompanied by new ways of assessing. A key concept here is what is called criterion-referenced assessment. Here performance is measured against criteria (descriptions of learning outcomes or objectives), not against the norms for the age group or class. The emphasis is on attainments and mastery. Within a course, learning objectives are set. Often there are key concepts, key skills, key facts and understandings, which form a core. All pupils are expected to master these, and demonstrate their mastery through their performance. Some will no doubt have problems, and diagnostic tests are used to identify pupils who have difficulty in coping, and where they are experiencing problems.

Remediation will be offered. Pupils who successfully master the core will usually be offered extensions which increase their skills, deepen their understandings, extend their knowledge and follow their own interests.

Those using criteria (descriptions of intended learning outcomes) often prefer continuous assessment (assessment throughout the learning period not necessarily non-stop, but as an organic part of the teaching/learning). They will emphasise the feedback to students possible in formative assessment, where assessment is seen as contributing to learning, rather than a judgemental summing up at the end of learning.

You will find a detailed discussion of criterion-referencing in Chapter 7. This is followed by a discussion of examinations in Chapter 8.

Summary: Frames of Reference

The two approaches – norm-referenced assessment (typically, end-of-course examination designed to produce a rank order) and criterion-related assessment (often in the form of continuous assessment with an emphasis on formative assessment) – can, and often do, co-exist. Some feel that they are complementary approaches, both of value at different points in the pupil's career. Some would modify the traditional examination to take cognisance of the new thinking; for example, in some schools experiments are taking place in 'open book' examinations (where pupils can bring in reference books, dictionaries and notes), or examiners are attempting to pay more attention to assessing higher order thinking skills, creativity and so on, possibly through an element of continuous assessment. Although some reformers have such a poor opinion of public examinations that they would abolish them, most teachers acknowledge that they must be accepted as a fact of life, but (argue some) it is not necessary for them to dominate the curriculum and assessment.

Which assessment strategy or strategies you adopt – a strategy based on norm-referencing and formal examinations, or criterion-referencing and (probably) continuous assessment – will depend on many factors. An important consideration is the question of validity and reliability since invalid and unreliable assessment is pointless. Validity and reliability is the subject of the next chapter.

3

Validity and Reliability

Much of what is said in this chapter may appear to be self-evident and much of it is reinforced in other chapters. None the less, concepts of validity and reliability are of such fundamental importance to all programmes of assessment and testing that it seems important to state exactly what they mean and look at areas where they must be closely considered.

What is Validity?

Validity really has two aspects. First, is what you expect your pupils to learn and do justifiable and reasonable? Second, do the methods of assessment achieve what they set out to do?

For many teachers both the syllabus and the assessment programme is decided for them by such external factors as 'O' level syllabuses. Teachers are simply not in a position to question the validity of a course or even the methods of testing. However, external examination syllabuses are only one aspect of a school curriculum. Increasingly, with such changes as the plans for 16+, teachers are being asked to develop wider approaches to teaching, learning and assessment. Before embarking on this you should ask yourself the following questions.

What are the aims of the course and its assessment? Is it to test mastery in a particular area of knowledge or a skill? Is it to diagnose a weakness and thus help a pupil achieve better? Is it to establish a rank order? Is it to indicate to prospective employers a range of skills and abilities and personality characteristics? As the answers to these questions vary, so the valid form of assessment will vary. To help decide which is the most relevant form you can look more closely at different types of validity.

Curricular Validity

The validity of courses (curriculum validity) is not the subject of this book. Nevertheless, unless you have a clear idea of what are the learning outcomes you expect – and feel reasonably confident that such learning outcomes are justifiable – you will not be able to make a valid assessment. You therefore need to make a statement about the course objectives: what you intend your pupils to be able to do at the end of the course. For example, in the 'O' level History course the aims are to help the pupils to:

(i) develop skills of analysis, judgement and empathy;

(ii) understand people of a different time and place; appreciate the diversity and continuity of human developments; understand change, causation and motivation.

(iii) understand their present world.

(iv) develop an interest in the past as a leisure pursuit.

A second example (Figure 3.1) is taken from the much more detailed objectives of a Schools Council modular course in Technology.

Construct Validity

Basically, construct validity means that in constructing a test or assessment you must be sure that it tests what it sets out to test and not something else. For example, if you want to assess manual dexterity and nothing else then the test or observation must not be blurred by including skills such as listening, or reading engineering drawings, and attitudes such as initiative or good motivation. Similarly, it is invalid to use essay questions in, say, a Physics or History examination if you have never taught your pupils how to write a good essay answer within your subject. Of course it may be impossible to achieve construct validity absolutely, none the less it should be noted. In cognitive areas (thinking skills) this theoretically should not be too difficult to achieve. Nevertheless, while a great deal of testing is done of what are classed the lower cognitive skills (such as recall of factual information) many assessment programmes fail to assess the higher cognitive skills: the ability to make inferences, to extrapolate, to interpret factual information, seeking meaning and unifying concepts (the skills of analysis and synthesis). Yet the higher cognitive skills are curricular objectives in most carefully-thought-out courses.

Specific Aims: Problem-solving

This module places emphasis on the process of technology rather than on the resources, knowledge and constraints which influence and affect the process. *The Energy Resources* and *Materials Technology* modules concentrate on these latter aspects. Its specific aims, therefore, are to help pupils:

(a) develop the capacity to analyse specific problems – to isolate the relevant factors in a problem and to establish a technique to evaluate alternative solutions to a given problem;
(b) be aware of the special needs of different sections of the community and the problems facing both the developed and developing countries;
(c) develop an ability to communicate effectively and efficiently orally, mathematically and scientifically, as well as by the written word, the use of drawing and by analogy;
(d) develop qualities of leadership and teamwork;
(e) combine scientific analysis with practical skills to produce an artefact, using the problem-solving process;
(f) develop an awareness of the need for safety in handling equipment as well as for any hardware they make to operate safely;
(g) become stimulated and motivated by creating an attitude of inquiry into aspects of technology;
(h) develop the ability to use the knowledge they have acquired from the *Energy Resources* and *Materials Technology* modules to solve complex problems (where these two modules have been taken by pupils);
(i) develop an understanding of processes and the use of machines and instruments;
(j) develop the ability to use hand tools and perform associated operations safely.

Source: Schools Council Modular Course in Technology: *Problem Solving* (Edinburgh: Oliver & Boyd, 1983).

Figure 3.1 Problem-solving module, 'O' level technology course

In the affective area – the area of feeling, of motivation, initiative, aesthetic appreciation and social and moral values – there is even more of a problem. Researchers have had great difficulty in establishing construct validity. So have schools and teachers. What should be assessed? And how can this be done without being highly subjective? (For further information see chapter 9.)

Criterion-related Validity

As the whole shape of education changes, particularly for 16+ pupils, so construct valdity must be re-examined. One way of checking this is to look at criterion-related validity. In the previous chapter the differences between criterion-related assessments and norm-related assessment has already been discussed.

For assessment in the cognitive area the criteria are often fairly straightforward: one teacher's measurement of a pupil's attainment in mathematics is not likely to differ from another's. However, in other areas and subjects this may be much more difficult. For example, English essays are notoriously difficult to validate (see Chapter 5).

Retrospective and Predictive Validity

The validity of assessment can be either retrospective (that is, you are measuring past performance) or predictive (measured against expected future performance). This latter is very difficult to establish, but is very commonly used in schools, for example when selecting pupils for a certificate course, filling in an UCCA form for university entrance and so on. At first glance it would appear that predictive validity would be relatively easy to establish in cognitive areas and more difficult in other areas. However, some research has shown that teachers' assessment of non-cognitive characteristics has more predictive value than academic cognitive validity: prediction of achievement is clearly difficult; success (or lack of it) may have more to do with motivation than abilities. But many decisions are based on the assumed predictive value of examinations or assessment: taking up a new subject – economics or a second language; making 'O' and 'A' level choices; selection for employment or university. These decisions are based on performances that may bear little resemblance to the course the student will embark upon.

However it is *content validity* which affects most teachers most of the time. Assessment must reflect the content and balance of the teaching that has gone before, and the objectives of the course. A test must ask only for what is expected, not more. For example if a class has been taught three reasons for the First World War it would then be invalid to ask for five reasons or give credit for them. Similarly if a Science teacher in a lesson on the telescope spends more time emphasising Galileo than the telescope then it would be invalid to test about the telescope and not Galileo. Testing must be compatible with the teaching method. For instance if essay writing has not been taught then it it is invalid to use it as an assessment tool. If the teaching method has stressed practical work then the assessment must reflect this. The oral assessment of a practical project will probably be more valid than a written test.

Content validity is particularly important in relation to criterion-referenced as opposed to norm-referenced assessment. If your intention in making an assessment is to rank pupils in order of ability or aptitude, you may perhaps include parts of the course work only covered by the ablest pupils in the top sets; other pupils may be unable to answer such questions because they have made slower progress. On the other hand the approach in criterion-referenced learning is that all pupils will have mastered the core (though obviously some may have gone further). Figure 3.2 is an example of a criterion-related attainment test in oral French. Note how the pupil is made aware of exactly what he/she must be able to do to pass. (In all there were 95 objectives for these third-year pupils.)

To ensure content validity you have to be sure that the criteria you are aiming for are validly taught before being tested. Then, referring to your objectives, decide the weighting you wish to give to each. You can then draw up the test and plan its content. One way of doing this is to draw up a specification grid. In this you decide what it is you want to test, and the importance you wish to place on each question. One side of the grid is made up of skills and abilities; the other, of the information. Then you can weight the marks accordingly (see Fig. 3.3).

Oral assessment, to supplement, or follow up the assessment of written work, can greatly improve the validity of assessment. Certain forms of written assessment put a premium on the recognition of correct information (for example, in spotting the correct response in a multi-choice question) or Mastermind-type recall (certain 'O' level papers, evidence suggests, can be passed simply by learning notes by rote). Oral assessment, however, provides valid opportunities to find out when a pupil shines, why a child is failing, or where he or she is getting by on half-understood but well-memorised notes. It may also provide opportunities denied in written work – perhaps because the pupil is weak in that area – to assess the pupil's grasp of core concepts.

Reliability

If a test is completely valid it should also be reliable. What is reliability? First, a reliable assessment enables you to make reliable comparisons. The comparisons may be between the performance of different pupils (norm-related reliability) or between the pupil's attainment and the course objectives (criterion-related reliability). Second, reliability is consistency. How far would the same test give the same result if done by the same children under the same conditions? Clearly this is an impossible situation to achieve absolutely. There will always be some variables.

Basic Objectives in Spoken French

Before taking your Stage 3 attainment test, here is a chance for you to test yourself and your partner.

If you can do all of these objectives quickly, competently and accurately in spoken French, you have an excellent chance of passing your speaking test at the highest level.

Your teacher will give you a checklist of possible ways of doing these objectives in French. You and your partner should test each other, then refer to this checklist to see how well you have done. We suggest a target number of phrases or sentences that you should try to produce for each objective. This is only a very rough indication – in many cases you may be able to go far above the target number.

OBJECTIVE	Target number of phrases or sentences
1 Talking about names	6
2 Talking about nationality	6
3 Talking about your home town	
– which town you live in	
– what type of town it is	3
– whether you like it	3
– what leisure facilities it has	8
– number of inhabitants	1
– whether it is twinned with another town	1
– where it is situated	1
– where you live in the town	1
– what people can do there	8
Saying where other people live, and talking about their home towns	10
4 Talking about how old people are	6
5 Greeting people	
– in casual spoken language	1
– in more formal spoken language	2
– in a letter to a friend or relative	1
6 Leaving people	
– in casual spoken language	1
– in more formal spoken language	2
– in a letter to a friend or relative	1
7 How are you?	
– asking and saying how you are	10
– asking and saying what hurts	10

Source: *Tour de France*, book 3 (London: Heinemann Education Books, 1983).

Figure 3.2

Early nineteenth-century factory conditions

	Child labour	1833 Act	Economic arguments	Total
Factual recall	3	5	2	10
Interpretation	3	1	1	5
Discussion	1	1	3	5
	7	7	6	20

Figure 3.3 Specification grid

First, there are the human factors. For example, a child will have forgotten or remembered something; health may affect a child's performance, so can what happened at home that morning, even the temperature of the room. Perhaps very little can be done about this, but it should be noted. Teachers, too, are subject to influence such as health and domestic problems. A teacher marking his 100th examination script will probably mark it a lot less reliably than the first. Handwriting can affect reliability, as can the teacher's personal feelings about a child.

Objective testing is one way of overcoming some of these variables (especially subjectivity) and achieving greater reliability. However, objective tests in some circumstances would reduce validity, and even at best they, like any other test, can only sample a small part of a pupil's knowledge.

Probably the greatest conflict between validity and reliability comes in the area of essay writing. An objective test, while it may be the most valid and reliable way to test knowledge and recall, is the least valid way to assess a pupil's ability to analyse, synthesise and evaluate. The most valid way to assess these higher cognitive skills may be through essay writing – and this can be highly unreliable. There is more on this point in the chapter on extended writing (Chapter 6).

Summary

Fundamentally you must decide what your aims are, what the course is trying to do and what the purpose of the assessment is. We have to accept that no assessment can be completely valid or completely reliable. However, once you are aware of the likely areas of unreliability, you can take steps to reduce them.

	Thinking skills		Communication	Other objectives		PSYCHO-MOTOR SKILLS, e.g. manual dexterity	Comments and Recommendations
	Recall of course content Factual information Knowledge	Higher cognitive skills: analysis, synthesis, evaluation, e.g. creative thinking, generating and solving your own problems	Reading, writing graphical, statistical, etc.	AFFECTIVE: concerned with feelings and relationships, e.g. motivation, empathy	AESTHETIC: appreciation of beauty		
Objective tests, e.g. multi-choice questions (Chapter 5)	V: Sampling: very good, though often superficial R: good Appropriate	V: often poor R: often poor Not recommended	Writing often very limited Reading, etc.: depends on questions	Not recommended	Not recommended irrelevant	Irrelevant	Use as *part* of an assessment strategy to sample course content. Questions must be very carefully and professionally constructed; it must be relevant to course content. Routine marking attractive.
Short answer questions/structural questions (Chapter 6)	V: Sampling – good/fair R: good/fair Appropriate	V: fair/poor R: fair/poor Limited use	Limited	Not recommended	Not recommended	Irrelevant	Both objective tests and structural questions can trivialise learning and make responses routine.
Comprehension exercises (Chapter 6)	Limited V: fair/poor R: fair/poor	V: good to very poor R: fair to poor	Writing limited, unless comprehension is very well-constructed	Possible V: uncertain R: poor	Possible V: uncertain R: poor	Irrelevant	Comprehension exercises often trivialise learning and make responses routine. Often over-used.
Extended writing, essays (Chapter 6)	V: poor R: poor Not recommended	V: fair/good but R: poor Appropriate	V: fair if backed with formative assessment R: fair	Possible V: uncertain R: uncertain	Possible V: uncertain R: uncertain	Irrelevant	Use as *part* of an assessment strategy to develop higher cognitive skills. Formative assessment essential at some stage. Marking difficult: tends to be subjective and time-consuming: use profile with projects.
Projects, field work extended assignments (Chapter 7)	V: poor R: poor Not recommended	V: fair/good but R: unproved Appropriate Recommended	V: fair if backed with formative assessment Recommended	Possible V: uncertain Motivating	Possible V: uncertain R: uncertain	Depends on nature of project	Projects recommended particularly for the development of information skills - planning, research, presentation.
Practical Projects	V: fair/poor R: fair/poor Usually inappropriate. Oral rather than written responses may be better	V: depends on project: can contain problem solving. R: depends on project	V: depends on project R: depends on project Oral assessment may be appropriate	Motivating	Only relevant if design element is included	V: fair/good R: fair/good Appropriate	Essential in practical subjects. Use profile as a basis for observation. Test recall.
Oral assessment a. a foreign language	V: fair/good R: fair/good	V: fair/good R: fair/good	V: fair/good R: fair/good	Possible	Possible V: subjective	Irrelevant	Oral assessment is essential in foreign languages. The use of profiles improves V and R. Use in formative assessment especially in project work, learning experiences, etc.
b. other subjects	Informal: fair Formal: very time consuming	Informal/supplemented by project work, etc. V: fair/good	Supplement to written work: improves V	Possible V: subjective			
Profiles specifying learning objectives (Chapter 11)	See comments						Profiles (or a check list of intended learning outcomes) can be used as a part of most assessment strategies.

Figure 3.4

Use methods of assessment which fit the teaching methods. There should be variety and balance. Choose the most appropriate tools. Figure 3.4 gives a summary of the validity and reliability of various assessment techniques (for example, objective tests, essays, and so on) in relation to intended learning outcomes.

PART II
SOME ASSESSMENT TECHNIQUES

4

Objective Testing

In this chapter we look at what is meant by objective tests, outline some procedures for their construction and marking, and discuss some of the advantages and disadvantages of using them.

What are Objective Tests?

What is an objective test? Simply, an objective test is a test which is free from any subjective bias - either from the tester or the marker. (Confusingly in education jargon, the adjective 'objective' usually means 'not subjective', while the noun 'objective' usually means an aim, a goal, target or intention. This chapter is not about course objectives - aims, intended learning outcomes, etc. - but about testing which is free from subjective elements.) There can only be one right or objective answer to such an objective test. Objective tests can take various forms, but invariably they require brief answers with little or no writing. A simple tick or a quick oral answer may be enough.

Let's take a look at some of the different types of objective testing.

First - and very commonly used by teachers as part of their day-to-day teaching - is simple recall. The teacher asks a short question, expecting a quick one-word answer or a simple statement completed.

Examples: Simple Recall

i.	*Direct question*	-	In what battle was Napoleon finally defeated?
ii.	Expected answer	-	Waterloo
iii.	*Incomplete statement*	-	A writer called Jane..............wrote *Pride and Prejudice*.
	Expected answer	-	Austen

Rather more complex than tests for simple recall are the following types of question which I have grouped under the heading: Choice–Response. These may be subdivided into the four varieties: multiple choice, true/ false, matching block, multiple completion.

(i) *Multiple Choice*
For the multiple choice the candidate must select what he thinks is the correct answer from a given list of possible answers:

Example: 'Any vessel or craft which may be proceeding towards Cuba may be intercepted.' Who, in 1962, issued this threat?

> a. Fidel Castro
> b. John F. Kennedy
> d. Richard Nixon
> d. Nikita Khruschev

The directive part of a multiple-choice question, giving information or instructions, is known as the stem. The key is the correct answer and the wrong options are the distractors.

In the preceding example the key is b. John F. Kennedy, while a, and c, and d, are distractors.

To answer the question a candidate would underline b, or alternately, write b in a space provided.

(ii) *True/False*

In the True/False variety, a statement is given either in plain language or numerically. The candidate then has to decide whether it is true or false and indicate accordingly.

Example: True/False –

	True	False
If A = (0, 2, 4) and B = (0, 3, 5, 7) then $A \cap B = \emptyset$		

Expected answer – False

Here the probability of guessing a correct answer is as high as one in two.

(iii) *Matching Block*

This type of question involves the matching of one list against the contents of another to show correct relationships.

Examples: *List I   Seaports*   *List II   Rivers*

1. Hamburg	a. Douro
2. Liverpool	b. Rhine
3. Oporto	c. St Lawrence
4. Buenos Aires	d. Yangtze Kiang
5. Montreal	e. Plate
	f. Mersey
	g. Elbe

In the match panel below enter the letter from List II to indicate the river on which each of the seaports in List I are situated.

Seaport   River

1	
2	
3	
4	
5	

One list must have a greater number of items than the other to prevent correct answers being obtained by elimination. (In this case b and d are the surplus distractors.)

(iv) *Multiple-Completion*

This is a more elaborate version of the multiple-choice format. While there is still only one correct answer, the candidate may be required to select more than one of the options. He is, therefore, compelled to consider carefully each piece of information given before arriving at a decision.

These higher-order forms of objective questions can be used to test more than mere factual knowledge.

Example: After 1932 De Valera launched a 'Cold War' against Britain in which he took some of the following actions.
Which were they?

    i. He imposed economic sanctions on trade with Britain
   ii. He forbade Irish immigrants to come to Britain
  iii. He deprived the Irish Governor-General of his powers
  iv. He militarised the Ulster frontier
   v. He established separate citizenship for Eire

  a. i, ii. and iv
  b. i, ii and v
  c. i, iii and v
  d. ii, iii and iv
  e. iii, iv and v

Key is c. Distractors – a, b, d and e.

Another form of objective test is simple sentence or paragraph completion. The pupil may be asked to fill in the blanks with words or phrases taken from a given list. In the example shown in Figure 4.1 the pupils will be successful if he can recall factual information, understands this information, and has grasped the trends and sequences.

INDUSTRIAL REVOLUTION

The first industrial revolution began in ....*(name a country)*.........................., during the eighteenth century, The technology was based on .... power, which was produced by burning ....

    The industrial revolution soon spread through both Europe and north America, and .... , and to ....

    During the early part of the nineteenth century, Britain was nicknamed the ' .... of the world'. But by about 1880 both .... and .... had overtaken her. By then the second industrial revolution had begun. This was based on new inventions and discoveries, particularly on technologies based on .... and ....

Some words to help you – (Careful – not all are correct!)
Brazil, Britain, Canada, China, France, Germany, Italy, Russia, United States, coal, electricity, natural gas, nuclear energy, steam, oil, water power, factory, workshop, powerhouse, shopping centre.

Figure 4.1

Advantages and Disadvantages of using Objective Tests

One problem immediately presents itself with any form of choice response – that is, guessing. Instructions not to guess are impossible to enforce and it is equally impossible for a marker to tell whether answers have or have not been guessed. This is particularly true of True/False tests where a candidate has a 50/50 chance of making a correct guess.

To counter this it is possible to apply a correction formula to all raw scores: $S = R - W$ (where S is the correct score, R the number of correct responses and W the number of wrong responses). If this is done candidates should be told in advance. However, many would argue that it is not worth the time and effort to do this. Moreover a candidate who makes an intelligent guess deserves credit; while a candidate who guesses blindly is not likely to do well and will be penalised by other non-objective parts of the assessment.

However, there are several positive advantages in using objective tests.

Probably the most obvious advantage is the speed at which they can be marked. Marking doesn't need any special skills so can be done by anyone, including pupils who have just sat the test. Moreover, as questions are short and easily answered, knowledge of a large syllabus content can be sampled. By using such tests to sample content knowledge, there is time available to use other assessment techniques to test other skills. Objective tests also give an opportunity to pupils who are poor writers to demonstrate their knowledge without subjective elements creeping in. Teachers and test constructors find writing of objective tests can be difficult; but just because of this difficulty it means that tests tend to be carefully scrutinised and thus less subjective. It therefore follows that well-written objective tests are likely to be highly valid and reliable in testing recall of syllabus content.

However, objective tests are not appropriate for all occasions: whereas they are excellent for sampling knowledge it is much more difficult to construct them to test higher-order skills. They can never test written expression, or ability to argue in your own words. If well written, however, they can test higher order skills.

The over-use of objective tests at the expense of other forms of assessment may result in an assessment which can be biased and invalid. But probably the main disadvantage of objective tests is the difficulty in writing good ones. Just as well-written tests are highly valid, so badly written objective tests are highly invalid. So how can you set about writing a good one?

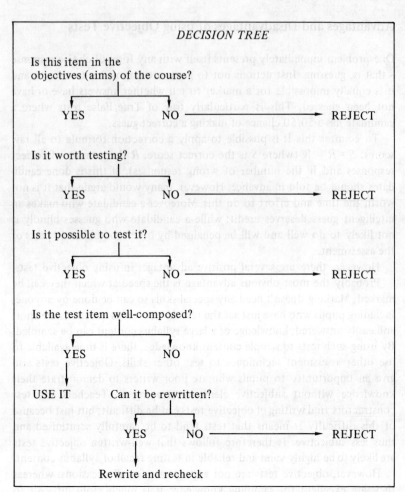

Figure 4.2

Writing Objective Tests

Before deciding what should be sampled through objective testing it is worth working through the decision tree shown below (Figure 4.2).

To answer the first stage look first at the objectives (aims) or criteria for the course and make sure your item is helping to test these. Exclude it if it doesn't. Keep the objectives (aims) in mind too when deciding whether the particular point is worth testing. It may be too trivial and could be answered by someone whether he has done the course or not. Just as you shouldn't put trivial items in, don't include an item which really cannot test what you expect it to. This may be particularly true of some higher-order skills – for example, understanding or analysis. You may think you are testing for understanding, but is it possible to answer the question purely by recognition? If that is so, either rewrite the item or use some other method of testing.

Now ask yourself, is the item well-composed and written? Is the key really correct? Are the distractors clearly incorrect? Can the correct answer be reached by elimination because the distractors are so trivial? Are the grammar, spelling and word order correct? Is the layout simple and unambiguous? Does it use positive rather than negative constructions? (Double negatives are especially misleading. Always underline **NOT** if you must use it.) Is the item understandable?

The most difficult objective tests to write are multiple-choice items. First let us look at what such an item contains. It is composed of:

The stem ——— 'Any vessel or craft which may be proceeding towards Cuba may be intercepted.' Who, in 1962, issued this threat?

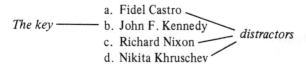

The key ———
a. Fidel Castro
b. John F. Kennedy
c. Richard Nixon
d. Nikita Khruschev

distractors

(The key is placed anywhere amongst the distractors, but vary its position from one question to another.)

Here is an example of a thoroughly bad multi-choice question, with most of the faults listed above. Try and answer it.

Example: Which of these is not required in writing a multi-choice question:

    i. subjective bias
    ii. pencil and rubber
    iii. does not fit the course objectives
    iv. no spelling mistakes or grammar
    v. plenty of time

Select your response from the following and tick the right answer space.

a. 1, 2 and 5   (Confusion of 1 and i)
b. None of the above   (Then Why ask?)
c. i. and ii. are correct (Implies the others may be too)
d. Only i. and ii. are correct

Answer: A B C D   (Confusion of A and a.
                          Confusion about where to place tick)

When all these points are considered it becomes apparent that there are many factors contributing to a good multiple-choice item. So that none are overlooked it is probably worth writing items along with colleagues. If this is not possible at least get others to check questions you write to find out the pitfalls. Pre-test them with pupils and be prepared to rewrite.

Writing good objective tests is a time-consuming business. However, as more and more teachers' gain practice in writing them so writing them becomes easier. And items which are proved useful can be added to an item 'bank'. These banks may exist at national level (with the examination boards) or at local level or within an individual department. There are also commercially produced books of objective questions. However, before using them teachers should be absolutely certain they are relevant to their particular course.

Conclusion

Finally, on planning any assessment strategy you should consider combining objective test-type questions with other forms of assessment to assess the whole range of skills from recall of information to understanding and analysis. On occasions a format akin to objective tests might be employed to ask questions about attitudes to other people, and open-mindedness to alternative hypotheses: there may be no 'right' objective answers. Does this mean that these questions should not be asked? How should the answers be marked? Finally, some skills cannot be tested by multi-choice techniques and here written responses should be used. They are an essential complement to objective testing.

It is to written responses that we now turn.

5
Written Responses: Essays, Guided Responses, Structured Questions

This chapter is concerned with how we use a whole range of written responses in assessment. In many subjects written work is the basis for most assessment. In almost all subjects the evidence for a pupil's success (or failure) is written evidence. Unless the pupil can successfully present what he has learned in a form in which we can assess it – and that often means a written form – neither pupil nor teacher can gauge the learner's progress and achievement.

The Choice of Assignments

The most immediate, practical choice before the working teacher is the choice of writing assigments. I begin here, not because other considerations are unimportant, but because this is where most teachers start.

Whether you teach 11-year-olds or sixth-formers you need to choose the form of stimulus, the shape of the question, the dimensions of the assignment for classwork, homework or examination. Whether you make up your own questions or use those at the end of a written textbook, you need to make decisions. Should you set a wide-open assignment or a tightly structured question? An essay, a comprehension exercise, a worksheet or a multi-choice test? There are a wide range of possibilities, as shown in Figure 1.3 of the opening chapter.

Let us begin at the most open end of the continuum. How non-directive should you be? How much freedom should you allow? How far can you expect your pupils to structure their own written response? Here are two open-ended assignments, both rather 'off-the-cuff' homework tasks, calling for *extended independent writing*:

For homework I want you to tell me all about our trip to the Tower of London today.

(Oral instruction to class of 11-year-olds)

What aspects of the political system in modern Sweden seem to be most worthy of comment?

(Blackboard – essay for sixth-form class)

The traditional examination *essay* question, usually more formal and more closely defined, also calls for extended writing:

Explain the political stability of modern Sweden

(End-of-term examination – sixth year)

What, to a biologist, are the seven key differences between living and non-living objects?

(Short essay set in end-of-unit assessment, 12-year-olds)

The next option is the *guided response*. The question or assignment provides clues to the organisation of the answer, or, in some cases, a check list of information to be included. For example:

Identify and discuss *three factors* that might help to explain the emergence of a stable political system in Sweden *despite* the massive social and economic changes engendered by the processes of modernisation. ('A' level question)

(Notice in this the clear directions: 'Identify and discuss . . . three factors . . . despite, . . . ') In the next example the teacher, working on the blackboard and using a question and answer routine with her class, arrived at the following outline:

Visit to Loch Sloy Hydro-Electric Power Station.

 i. Introduction. Purpose of visit.
 ii. Location of power station (include sketch plan).
iii. Main features:
　　valley before dam was constructed
　　dam and reservoir
　　　　　etc., etc.

(Fieldwork notes, 14-year-olds)

Another option is the *structured question*, or structured questionnaire. Many examination questions, and worksheets, call for short, limited answers:

A precise definition of life is not possible. We can, however differentiate between living and non-living objects. List the seven characteristics of living objects, and explain briefly the meaning of each term in relation (a) to plants and (b) to animals:

Characteristic	(a) *Plants*	(b) *animals*
1.	....	....
	....	....
	etc.	etc.

One form of this is the *comprehension exercise*. Comprehension tests have been widely criticised as trivial, irrelevant, misused and anti-education. The routine use of comprehension exercises is certainly a poor teaching/learning strategy. None the less, comprehension tests can be designed so that they are thought-provoking. Questions can be framed to assess learning objectives specified in terms of Bloom's taxomomy. Now turn to the very different, controversial comprehension examination on a descriptive passage about a stormy sea battering the beach (Figure 5.1). This is of great interest because two versions appear, one using open-ended questions, the other objective questions (multi-choice).

Fig. 5.1 Follows

PASSAGE I
Read the following passage then answer questions 1–5 from the question paper.

'At the sea's edge I hesitated, warily letting the white tongues of the sea lick my ankles. It was cold. And as I stood on the edge of the world, listening to the dog-chained growling sea scrambling up the beach for a bone, I thought of the drowned, who slept in the feathery
5 fathoms below the watery grey and green eiderdown that was pulled back and fore by the two-time swell.

'Then, like a bull, I suddenly rushed into the sea and the matador waves slapped my belly familiarly and the cold whistled into my shattered breath before I dived into a taller wave, and rose and snorted,
10 and blew my nose, and spluttered in the water for a joke.'

(a) Open-ended questions

1 Why does the author use the expressions 'dog-chained' and
   'growling'?   (2)
2 Give two reasons why the author should use 'tongues' in this
   context. Why is it appropriate of the author to use 'white' in
   this context?   (3)
3 What effect does the author achieve by referring to the sea's
   edge as 'the edge of the world'?   (2)

Essays, Guided Responses and Structured Questions   *57*

4 Pick out from paragraph I two words which continue the notion that the drowned are only asleep. (2)

5 Why does the author compare the waves to a matador? (2)

(b) Alternative version, using multi-choice questions (objective tests)

1 The sea is described as 'dog-chained' and 'growling' (line 3) to suggest that

A its noise resembles a dog's barking for its freedom
B the sea is a menace to man unless it is controlled
C the sea seems angry in being restricted in its passage up the beach
D the sea is no more controllable than a fierce dog is
E the sea is liable to injure anyone within its range.

2 The pairing of 'white' and 'tongues' (line 1) is justifiable because

A white, a symbol of cold, applies both to the sea and to a dog's tongue
B the metaphor of a dog's tongue relates to the shape and movement of the waves; the colour is that of the waves themselves
C the sea is said to be wary of licking his ankles and white symbolises fear
D the whiteness of the man's ankles is reflected in the lapping waves
E white is used as a metaphor of innocence; tongues as a metaphor of shape and movement.

3 In lines 2–3 the author calls the place he is standing the 'edge of the world' rather than the seas's edge (line 1). The effect of this is to

A avoid repetition of the same phrase
B suggest his fear of drowning
C achieve a pun on the word 'edge'
D convey a sense of desolation
E make us think of the end of the world.

4 The words 'feathery' and 'eiderdown' (lines 4 and 5) suggest that

A the moving tides provide a soft covering for the resting dead
B the sea was like a bird with its downy feathers extended
C the bottom of the sea was covered with moving seaweed
D drowned men rested on the soft sea-bed
E the green sea is like the grassy covering of a grave.

5 The writer uses the term 'matador waves' (line 7) to suggest that

A the sheets of water moved like a matador's cloak
B the waves hit him as the swords hit the bull
C the sea is fighting against him
D the waves keep coming at him, teasing him
E the sound of the waves resembled the swishing of a matador's cloak.

Source: *The Use of Multi-Choice Techniques in the Testing of Interpretation and Language Skills in English*
(Scottish Certificate of Education Examination Board, 1975).

Figure 5.1 Comprehension exercise

Finally we come to the *objective test*. Here the pupil may simply supply an answer consisting of a word or short phrase, or insert words on a sheet using the Cloze procedure, or, in the case of *multi-choice questions*, simply tick the appropriate box as in Figure 5.2(b). (Objective tests were discussed in the previous chapter.)

These are all valid approaches, useful as part of an assessment strategy.

Written Responses within an Assessment Strategy

The choice of assignment must, inevitably, depend on your assessment strategy. Here, for example, is a part of a plan drawn up by a teacher working with a class of 16-year-olds (Figure 5.2). The topic was Energy, and she was concerned with two main fields of knowledge:

i. Factual information on the different types of energy source:
   a. renewable sources, e.g. solar, wind and tidal power;
   b. non-renewable sources, e.g. wood, gas, oil, coal, etc.
ii. Consideration of the social, economic and environmental implications of energy needs, energy sources, energy shortages, and side effects, e.g. pollution

---

ASSESSMENT PROGRAMME: UNIT IV (ENERGY SOURCES)

	Assessment	*Objective*
Week 1	Worksheets, using structured *questions*. Marked by pupils, then handed in for check.	To structure, sequence and check on lessons 1 and 2: basic information.
Week 3	*Multi-choice test*. Marked by pupils. Pupils mastering core proceed to extension work; rest do remedial loop.	To check on mastery of core: a. renewable energy sources; b. non-renewable sources.
Week 5	*Guided response* assignment. Preceeded by oral work. Supported by formative assessment.	To develop concepts of social, economic and environmental considerations. *Aim*: to apply core information, to analyse and evaluate it.
Week 10	End of unit assessment:	
	a. *Multi-choice* paper and *structured questionnaire*.	To sample recall of course content.
	b. *Comprehension exercise:* extract from *New Scientist*.	To assess ability to make inferences.
	c. *Essay* question on energy and economic growth.	To assess ability to think logically and creatively.

Figure 5.2

This assessment strategy (of which Figure 5.2 is only a part) shows a flexible, planned approach, related to course objectives. First, the teacher ensured that she had regular feedback on her pupils' progress: she used worksheets and multi-choice questions. She was responsible for preparing her pupils for a public examination, so she gave regular practice in examination-type questions. This was supported in the learning stages by formative assessment. (This is discussed in detail later in this chapter.) At the end of term the pupils sat a practice examination in class time.

There were also longer-term objectives. 'It is not just a question of what my pupils ought to know, for examination purposes, about this topic. Nor is it simply my aim to train them to present what they know under examination conditions. I also have to ask how, through my subject, my pupils can develop the skills and competencies relevant to adult life, and understandings of themselves and their world.'

These skills and competencies depend to an important extent, on pupils' thinking skills, study skills and language skills. These are necessary for success in school, and are perhaps the most valuable resource pupils take away from school.

Thinking Skills

The development of thinking skills is clearly central to learning. The kinds of written responses we ask our pupils to produce must depend on the kinds of thinking skills we are seeking to develop:

	EXTENDED WRITING		SHORT ANSWERS	
	Free writing and essays	Guided responses	Structured questions	Objective tests
Recalling facts concepts, etc. (course content)	Not appropriate. Use other techniques.	Poor	Useful and appropriate	
Understanding and application of facts, concepts, etc.	Not appropriate	Limited usefulness	Useful and appropriate	Useful and appropriate, though somewhat limited
Analysis of facts, concepts – making inferences, etc.	Appropriate	Useful and appropriate	Limited use	Not appropriate: too limited
Synthesis and evaluation: creative thinking, generating own problems and solutions	Useful and appropriate	Appropriate training	Not appropriate: too structured and limited	

Based on Bloom's Taxonomy

Figure 5.3

Even young children can and do use high-level skills. Babies learn to speak, 6-year-olds to read. The acquisition of language, both spoken and written, calls for advanced skills: the ability to analyse language, to make and test hypotheses, to evaluate the meaning and effect of language. Educational psychologists have shown that although young children are not at home with abstraction they nevertheless do organise and learn from experiences. This ability improves with practice.

If we return to the assessment strategy adopted by the teacher dealing with the unit on Energy (Figure 5.2), we can see how she chose a variety of written assignments to develop and assess various levels of thinking.

In the past, many subject teachers assumed that the assessment of the course content – what the pupil knows about, say, History of Physics – can be language-independent. The way the pupil wrote was 'English', and irrelevant. The teacher's job was to ignore the 'English', and mark the recall of course content and the pupils ability to organise the information.

Thinking, however, is almost inseparable from language. Teaching takes place through language, as does learning. The only way we can assess what has gone into our pupils' heads, and what they have made of it, is through language. The most practical way to assess their learning is through language 'fixed' on paper: writing.

Language Skills

The Bullock Report on *Language across the Curriculum* has drawn the attention of all teachers to the fact that success in *all* school subjects is, to a large extent, success in the language of the subject. Although we can think without language (as when we play chess, go fishing or listen to music) most advanced thinking is dependent on language. Language, particularly written language, presents the most visible indication of thought. When we assess a pupil's written work we are assessing his skills in using language, written language, to mediate his thinking – what is going on in his head: the way he recalls what he has learned, whether he has integrated it with what he learned earlier, how he 'fixes' it on the page.

The spoken word is extremely important. Writing is almost impossible if you do not rehearse what you are going to write, either aloud or in your head. In everything that follows I assume a great deal of oral work. But assessment of oral work is extremely difficult, often subjective and always time-consuming. Inevitably assessment depends to a large extent on the written evidence in most subjects.

If you think language matters in your subject, should you assume a responsibility for it? There is often a great deal of head-shaking in the staffroom over the 'appalling' handwriting, spelling or English of today's first years, or sixth years. 'They just do not seem able to turn out a well-planned essay' is the complaint. The message of the Bullock Report is that this is everyone's responsibility. But how do you raise standards through your assessment procedures?

Technical Competence and 'Fitness for Purpose'

A 'language across the curriculum' profile may offer a way forward. Here is a profile developed to be used *once* a term in every subject Figure 5.4. It was recommended as the basis for a joint assessment by pupil and teacher of one extended piece of writing.

Pupil's name...

Class...

Subject..

Writing task...

....

....

		Outstanding	Good for purpose of task	Adequate for purpose of task	Inadequate for purpose of task	Serious general weakness
TECHNICAL COMPETENCE	Handwriting and presentation					
	Spelling – general and special vocabulary					
	Punctuation					
	Grammatical skills					
	Handling of sentence and paragraph structures					
	Use of vocabulary – general and specialist					
FITNESS FOR PURPOSE	Sense of audience and function					
	Organisation and structure					
	Coverage of content i. .... ii. .... iii. .... iv. .... v. .... etc.					

Figure 5.4

Assessment: From Principles to Action

It is easiest to use such a profile where there are agreed standards for technical competence within a school language policy. What happens in Geography is then reinforced by the standards being set in Science and in English. Even in schools where there is no such policy, departments or individual teachers can adopt a profile. It may be helpful in a department for all the teachers to mark a few photocopied scripts, using the profile, and then discuss their findings.

Pupils need to be involved in the exercise, otherwise they can derive little benefit. Hence the importance of concentrating, for a week or two, on formative assessment (assessment which takes place alongside, and in support of, the learning process). A busy teacher cannot be expected to mark in great detail every script, every spelling mistake, every missing punctuation mark. The pupil himself has to learn these editing skills. Pupils working in pairs, editing each other's work, often can improve standards.

The technical competence of almost all pupils improves if they are given insights into what is expected of them, particularly if this is followed with guidance on how to improve. Regular practice and regular assessment reinforce the message. The same is true of performance in a task as they develop the concept of 'fitness for purpose'.

A case in point was a class of 11-year-olds where the profile was used alongside a project. The class had been involved in a cycling proficiency course, and were now producing a *Which?* guide to buying bicycles. Each child had to evaluate the bike of his choice. They were used to producing material for their teacher (the commonest audience in school; the next most common is the pupil himself), but they needed help to understand that in the project their *audience* was different. This involved them in considering the *function* of their report. What would their readers – would-be bicycle owners and their parents – want or expect? Was this the place for a poem? a story about themselves? Clearly not. The job was one calling for factual information. This required *organisation and structure*. The model they followed was that of consumer publications, but the format had to be adapted to the task. Lastly, the *content* was vital. They listed, on the profile, items to be covered – design, safety, maintenance, value for money and so on.

In the case of this *Which Bike?* project, assessment took place informally during the writing *process*. The process included the pupils writing a brief for the investigation, deciding on criteria for consumer choice, and making decisions about layout. All these involved questions about 'fitness for purpose' The process culminated in drafting, editing and writing a fair copy for display as a wall magazine. Here technical competence was important. The *product* (the finished work) was assessed by the group. (For more discussion of projects see Chapter 6.)

Intelligent children often seem able to learn the hidden ground rules of the assessment game. Less able and less mature children often fail to grasp the rules. In particular they have problems with understanding what is appropriate to the task. The problems are twofold: problems with writing and, even more basic, problems with understanding the difference between transactional and expressive language.

Transactional language is the language that we use to get things done: to convey a message, to communicate information. This is the language that we teachers usually require in school work. Yet the structured, objective functional language of learning, of textbooks and of examinations is a very difficult, and very unattractive, language for immature youngsters. If you listen to most children talking, you will hear them using what is called '*expressive* language'. This is the language which is 'close to the self' – the unstructured language which readily reveals and expresses the flow of thoughts and feelings. They describe events, people and objects in terms of their own perceptions, feelings and reactions.

Even as late as the mid-teens, many youngsters are still having difficulties with transactional language. If we want them to be able to describe events and objects clearly and objectively they need to develop transactional language. A solution, adopted by many teachers, is to provide pupils with only limited opportunities for using their own words. Oral work is reduced. Notes are dictated. No opportunities are given for extended writing; instead multi-choice questions and short answers to structured worksheets are the norm.

Disquiet has been expressed about this on two grounds. First, the elimination of all personal and expressive elements may be demotivating. It devalues personal experience, and the uniqueness of the individual. It negates experiential learning. Could this account, in part, for the deterioration too often found in the written work of less able pupils as they move up the secondary school? Second, the elimination of expressive elements may be a disservice to young writers. As adults, we look for that sparkle, that vividness, which comes from the writer's personal involvement and enthusiasm, even in books and articles on serious academic subjects. Without it, our attention wanders. Good writers are those who have learned to handle expressive elements in a mature way. It only comes with practice. Closely linked with the problems pupils experience in using transactional language rather than the more natural, personal expressive language, is the problems for many pupils of differences between written and spoken English. To many children 'examinationese' is a foreign language. Our culture depends to a great degree on the spoken word: it is the medium of normal social intercourse, of radio and television. The language of many children is very restricted and even oral communication, using transactional English, may be difficult. If they have any reading matter in ther homes, it may be confined to comics and the popular press (with all their problems; verbless sentences; knock-down phrases. Wham!). Such children need a great deal of help. One school of thought offers them many mechanical tasks (copying from textbooks, multi-choice questions, but no extended writing). Others argue that they need help in using their own words – to develop language and thinking skills – and that much (but not all) written work should be based on oral work, and be close to the pupil's own expressions. Only (it is argued) by using pupils' own perceptions, ideas, feelings and experiences, can pupils with serious writing problems be motivated to go through the process of drafting and redrafting to reach an acceptable standard.

Let us now look in greater detail at the advantages, and disadvantages, of various kinds of writing assignments. A sensible assessment strategy is likely to employ many different approaches, from the objective questions (for example, multi-choice questions) through structured questions and guided response to extended writing, structured by the pupil himself.

Structured Questions

The most efficient way of sampling course content widely is by using short-answer questions. Both structured questions and multi-choice questions are extremely efficient at testing recall, particularly recall of factual information. Multi-choice questions were discussed in the previous chapter.

Advantages and Disadvantages

Structured questions are a useful tool in almost every subject. By their nature such questions can help provide structure and sequence to learning experiences, and because of this are often used in structured worksheets, comprehension and interpretation exercises or questionnaires related to a particular topic. They are frequently used in the interpretation of diagrams, statistics, graphs, maps, etc. They are useful for diagnostic purposes because they can probe in exactly the areas that the assessor wants while still allowing sufficient flexibility of answer for the pupil to reveal the nature of his difficulty.

However, structured questions lose some, if not most, of their value in assessing the higher cognitive skills, the further they move in the direction of multi-choice and other forms of objective testing.

Two dangers should be guarded against: inappropriate or poorly constructed questions can trivialise, mislead or restrict; and the lure of marking routine answers can lead to over-use of this technique.

Writing Structured Questions

Figures 5.5(a) and (b) give examples of structured questions. As will be seen, a structured question has two main parts: the stem and the sub-questions.

Speaking in Brussels, a British government spokesman fiercely criticised the Common Agricultural Policy. He said that far too much of the Community Budget was spent on agriculture and, in particular, on supporting inefficient farmers. Much more must be done to divert resources to the Regional Fund, and to tackle the twin problems of declining industries and urban decay.

(From a recent newspaper report)

a. Give two reasons for Britain's criticism of the CAP:

i. .... (2 marks)

ii. .... (2 marks)

b. Name and briefly describe **one** project in your area which was funded from the Region Fund:

....

.... (4 marks)

c. Name three other EEC member states that would obtain greater benefit from an expansion of the Regional Fund. Give brief reasons for your answer.

Name of country   Reasons for benefiting

i. .... (3 marks)

etc.

Figure 5.5(a)   Structured questions

A pupil designed the following experiment to investigate the effect of light on the behaviour of the small fresh-water crustacean 'Daphnia'.

The tube was gently shaken until the 'Daphnia' were evenly distributed in the water (Diagram A).

Diagram B shows the redistribution of the 'Daphnia' after several minutes.

Diagram A   Diagram B

i. From the above observation the pupil concludes that the 'Daphnia' moved towards light.

State two ways in which the design of the experiment could have extended to support his conclusion. (2 marks)

1. ....

....

2. ....

....

ii. Suggest one other possible hypothesis to account for the distribution of 'Daphnia' in Diagram B. (1 mark)

....

....

iii. What term is used to describe the behaviour of the 'Daphnia' in the above experiment. (1 mark)

....

(Examples i and ii taken from SCE Higher Biology Paper I, 1974).

Figure 5.5(b) Structured questions

Essays, Guided Responses and Structured Questions 67

Stem

Although the stems in these examples are written, the sources of stems might be films, slides, tape recordings, tables of data, statistical diagrams, photographs, etc.

In tests stems can vary in length. They are usually kept short, although for comprehension/interpretation purposes they may be lengthy, even an entire chapter of a book. Often, however, the stem is edited by the writer of the question to remove irrelevant and superfluous material.

The stem information should determine the structure and sequence of the sub-questions. The nature of the stem also determines what skills and abilities the pupils require to respond to the materials (The sequence often is similar to the normal sequence of teaching.)

Sub-questions

The following points are considered good practice in writing sub-questions in tests:

i. There should be a logical sequence about the sub-questions.
ii. The sub-questions should be independent of one another so that a pupil can answer a later sub-question even if he has answered an earlier one incorrectly.
iii. The sub-questions should assist the pupil to understand the material, by drawing his attention to salient points.
iv. The pupils should be given guidance by being told the weighting of sub-questions (marks allotted).
v. The layout should allow adequate space for large writing, but encourage precise rather than verbose answers and generally give guidance about the length of the response required.

In writing sub-questions the purpose of the test must always be borne in mind. Thus, if the purpose of the test was to obtain a normal curve of distribution, the sub-questions might become progressively harder in level of difficulty; on the other hand, if the purpose was to test for minimum level of competency, the standard of the questions would be more uniform.

Interpretation/Comprehension Exercises

In comprehension exercises the pupil is presented with a stem which may be of considerable length: an article from the *New Scientist* or *The Econo-*

mist, a taped conversation in French, a complete poem, an extract from *The Times* in 1914. Increasingly, with the use of original source material in the social sciences, pupils are asked to examine documentary evidence and make inferences. The carefully written sub-questions can help to structure learning experiences. See Figure 5.1 (page 57).

Over-practice in this technique, particularly in English, leads pupils to a belief that there is a standard structure for responding to, say, a poem or short story. As with all structured questions, there are real dangers in the technique: learning is trivialised, made routine and superficial. The clever child can be taught by an astute teacher to respond with a cynical disregard for truth to questions about why he 'enjoyed' this poem: in an examination it is not acceptable to dislike the set poem, or to like it for reasons that are personal and extraneous to the poem.

Extended Writing: Essays and Guided Responses

Structured questions and multi-choice questions are a boon to teachers in that they are very easy to mark. The writing of worksheets, textbooks and tests which use standard questions has been a major growth area in education for several decades. These, clearly, are welcomed and used by teachers as a valuable aid to ensuring that the pupil has covered the syllabus and can recall key facts. Why then should we also use extended writing assignments in our assessment strategy?

The pupil's own writing provides him with the opportunity to explore, in his own words, what he has learned. The recognition of someone else's words (the ticking of a right answer in a multi-choice question) is only the beginning of an awareness of truth. It is only when the pupil has organised what he has learned, or explained it to someone else, that he really *knows*. Extended self-structured writing, moreover, provides opportunities for pupils to think creatively: to use their own personal experiences, perceptions, observations and understandings; to speculate, to make and test hypotheses; to identify problems, seek solutions, suggest remedies. In short, the pupil's own writing gives him opportunies denied in the limited structured responses required in worksheets and tests. This is the reason why essays continue to play such an important part in higher education, and in the selection procedures for higher education, at 'O' level and 'A' level. But, as I have argued before, all pupils, whatever their ability, need to develop their powers of thinking and writing, need to initiate, plan, organise and produce work, need to be valued for their own responses.

'Extended writing' is a term which I will use to cover all assignments which call for continuous writing – say, a page or more depednning on the pupil's age. It includes not only formal essays, but any writing structured by the pupil himself (possibly after oral discussion): journal writing, field-work reports, letters, imaginative reconstructions in history, as well, as much that is done in the English classroom. I shall use the term 'essay' to refer particularly to the kind of answer which is required in public examinations (or classwork preparatory to examinations).

The teacher's most immediate problem is how to assess extended writing. There are really two stages. First, formative assessment, assessment which takes place in support of, and alongside, the process of writing. Second, assessment for differentiation, which is used for ranking the performance of pupils in order of merit.

Formative Assessment

You almost certainly use formative assessment as part of your teaching already, though you may not label it as such. But you may feel that it is not 'proper assessment', and that all essays must receive a mark or grade which places them in rank order (assessment for differentiation). This, as we shall see, is demanding. An alternative is, with agreement from your pupils, to dispense occasionally with ranking, and concentrate for a week or two on formative assessment.

If you decide that your pupils need to learn how to produce a 'good' essay in your subject, then at some point fairly early in the course you might devote a block of time to formative assessment.

Formative assessment begins with helping the pupil sort out some central issues he needs to consider before undertaking any piece of extended writing:

i. What is the purpose of this writing? What (in an examination) is the point of the question? What does the question mean? What, implicitly or explicitly, are the guidelines, the parameters, the boundaries? (Pupils need considerable guidance on the terminology of questions.)
ii. What do I know about this topic? What resources do I have to answer this question? Do I need further information? If so, how do I get it? Of all the information I have, what is relevant? How do I select my facts? What do I include? What do I leave out?

iii. How do the facts, events, people, ideas, connect with each other? What is the internal logic, coherence or structure of the facts?
iv. What makes a 'good' essay within this subject area? What shape should I give my essay? How do I start off? What should be in my opening paragraph? What forms of language will be best for the effect I want to produce? How should I end?

Discussion and reflection help to clarify these issues, but they can only be learned through experience of repeated practice.

The discipline of planning, drafting, redrafting, editing and presenting written work is essential to clear thinking and effective writing. Few adults would attempt a serious piece of writing 'off the top of their heads'. Yet the examination hall demands this, and, to practise this skill all too many inadequate essays are thrown off during course work and later used as a basis for revision. In the scurry to cover the syllabus, pupils never get taught how to write and how to think.

Planning, drafting, rewriting and editing afford opportunities for the teacher to provide formative assessment for writing skills and thinking skills. Often this can usefully be extended by pupils working in pairs, using a profile (for example, the profile on Figure 5.4, p. 62). Pupils should be encouraged to read aloud any awkward passages to their partner: this is a good check on incoherence and poor thinking. They should edit carefully and then produce fair copies. Samples of the work can then be displayed on the classroom walls to illustrate teaching points about what makes a good essay. The point of an exercise like this is to encourage pupils to set their own standards, to be self-critical and to learn editing skills. Numerical marks are probably not useful: your verbal comments as you pin up examples are more effective.

Assessment for Differentiation

It is when we turn to assessment of essays for differentiation – assessment intended to produce a rank order of pupils – that we run into the most acute difficulties.

There are, undoubtedly, difficulties in assessing the thinking, writing and study skills that are at the centre of extended writing. They are difficult to assess rapidly. Assessment lacks the objectivity so easily available in marking multi-choice questions. Essays provide – or should provide – opportunities for pupils to think divergently, to be creative, to express individuality, to hypothesise and speculate. How do you mark fairly such divergence? And how do you assess essays in depth – valuing the well-marshalled arguments, perceptiveness or a good selection of facts – despite distractions such as poor spelling, or minor slips in factual information?

Validity and Reliability

Particularly in examinations, there are problems with validity and reliability. A valid assessment will be a valid test of the knowledge, skills and understandings to be assessed, and will make valid comparisons between candidates undertaking the same task. A reliable assessment will produce results which, if the candidates were to repeat a similar test, would be approximately the same.

So what happens in a public examination, or, indeed, in an examination at the end of the year? Not all the candidates have covered identical syllabuses, with identical teachers. So a choice of questions is offered. To make a valid comparison between candidates, however, all candidates should do the same compulsory questions. But this would be an invalid test of a candidate's knowledge (because it would not be a valid test of the syllabus) and unreliable (since the candidates who were lucky in the choice of question would do well this time, while others, equally intelligent and hardworking, might not).

The implications of this question of validity and reliability is discussed in detail in the section on sitting examinations in Chapter 3 (Validity and Reliability).

One problem with assessing essays validly and reliably is that it is very easy to make *subjective judgements*. The writing of a pleasant, obedient child may be ranked higher than that of an unattractive but clever pupil. This is known as the 'halo' effect. Moreover, it is very easy to give favourable assessment to views that echo your own values – for example, your taste in literature, your political attitudes in history or economics, even your enthusiasms in chemistry. Presentation and handwriting, also, have been shown to have a decided effect on marking.

Various strategies can be used both in marking examination papers and in marking essays done in the classroom or for homework.

A *marking scheme* can be adopted. This can make marking more objective. For example, when marking an essay you might decide on the following scheme:

In this case the 'content' might be determined by a checklist of the points you considered essential in such an essay, while 'structure' would be related to how the writer organised the information, and dealt with cause and effect, etc. If pupils know that you are using a marking scheme,

	Outstanding	Good	Inadequate	Serious problems
Spelling	3	2	1	0
Presentation	3	2	1	0
Handwriting and 'English'				
Structure	6	5	3	1
Organisation				
Development				
Content	8	6	3	1
Total	20	15	8	2

Figure 5.6

they often respond positively by producing work which more adequately meets your standards.

In examinations which may have important effects – for example, examinations which will decide which pupils can opt for an 'O' level course – standards need to be set within a department. Consultations are useful, as are multiple marking of sample scripts. A marking scheme may be used, or multiple marking, using 'impression' marking. 'Impression' marking is rapid marking done on impression rather than a careful check through every point in a candidate's answer. It is surprisingly consistent in factual subjects (e.g. Geography, Biology, etc.) if the examiners are experienced, and if the marks of two examiners are combined. Multiple marking may, however, be completely misleading in creative writing where one marker may give a poem or short story an A+ and another find the same piece of writing totally fails (for him) and will award an E−. Neither would award the average of a C. This is a major problem in English.

Conclusion

The strength of short-answer questions is their ability to sample the course curriculum widely, if somewhat superficially. The strength of extended writing is that it provides opportunities to develop thinking skills, especially the higher cognitive skills, and opportunities for experiential learning (learning based on the pupils' own experiences). This potential, however, will not be exploited unless positive steps are taken to use formative assessment to develop the thinking and language skills through regular practice.

In this chapter I have argued that no one form of written assessment is a valid assessment of the learning objectives we set for our pupils. We cannot, using only one form, assess the range of facts, concepts and arguments contained within a course, nor the skills and competencies developed by the course, including the all-important thinking and writing skills. We need the whole continuum of written assessment, from objective tests (multi-choice questions, Cloze procedure, etc.) through structured questions, and guided responses, to extended writing including essays, creative writing and possibly field work and projects. It is to the use of projects, and assessment of projects that we now turn.

6

The Assessment of Projects and Extended Assignments

Project work, whether individual or group work, presents special difficulty for assessment. A single holistic mark for the varieties of skills involved is clearly inappropriate. It does, however, provide an opportunity to assess a variety of skills and activities that are peculiar to project work.

This chapter is designed to show which skills and abilities are best assessed through project work, together with some of the techniques and problems of such assessment.

Project work can vary considerably in the time taken to produce the end-product. The kinds of skills involved often include project planning, research and retrieval, analysis and interpretation of data, as well as the practical and communication skills required to establish and present the final product.

These are not the kinds of skills normally presented for assessment. Yet they are frequently used in primary schools, and many examination boards now increasingly use project types of work as an important part of their overall assessment in certain subjects. Although projects are not as easily assessable as more formal kinds of work, the educationally valuable processes involved in them should not be reduced in significance, or dismissed by a single holistic mark, simply because of the difficulties involved.

The assignment and project approach is used by many subjects. Although each subject discipline approaches project work according to its own ethos, a common description of the basic objectives may be possible. It should, however, be noted that projects and assignments can promote diversity of the final product. This is unlike the more usual convergence towards a particular goal in other forms of assessment. While this may be educationally desirable, it does make assessment more difficult. However, it is clear that the assessment system must include all aspects of a subject which are considered educationally valuable; and must not just concentrate on those aspects which are easily assessed at the expense of those which present difficulties.

The best individual studies usually occur in circumstances where

i. A manageable problem is defined.
ii. A hypothesis or generalisation is advanced or a model formulated.
iii. Data are collected – by first-hand observation and research – even if quite limited.
iv. Data are analysed and presented by appropriate techniques.
v. Conclusions are reached which enable the hypothesis, generalisation and model to be evaluated.

Projects are normally assessed as part of the internal syllabus. But there is an increasing element of external assessment/moderation of such forms as 'special study' in Modern Studies, dissertation in Geography, Science, etc., and it seems clear that as internal assessment becomes more prevalent the project/assignment may be an appropriate vehicle for school-based assessment.

Teachers can adopt a variety of approaches to the assessment of school-based projects. Assessment can be entirely *subjective*, based not on any criteria, but the teacher's intuitive 'feel'. This does not usually produce valid or reliable assessments or useful feedback to pupils. An alternative is to *rank* the end-product (the project report). Usually in a class of, say, twenty-five pupils, three or four project reports will stand out as being well above the general standard, and a similar number will fall far below the average. The middling project reports can then be arranged roughly into grades B and C. This is still unlikely to give pupils any feedback about why one report is better than another, and how their reports could have been improved.

Other more useful approaches are possible. First, I would like to discuss two methods of using *formative assessment* (assessment which supports learning). After this, I will be discussing *performance assessment*. Finally, I will be looking at *assessment related to objectives*.

Formative Assessment

Formative assessment can usefully take place during the process of project work. Figure 6.1 shows an Individual Study Strategy Sheet, which was used by a pupil to plan his strategy. The teacher (and pupil) have assessed the strategy formatively: that is to say, they consulted together and only after a second draft, when an adequate strategy had been worked out, did the student receive the 'go-ahead'.

INDICATIONAL STUDY STRATEGY SHEET

INDIVIDUAL STUDY STRATEGY SHEET   1st, 2nd, 3rd draft

To be completed by .... (date) after consultation with

.... (teacher's name).

NAME .... Tutor group ....

OUTLINE PROPOSAL

General area of interest:

Possible title:

Aim of study:

WORKING STRATEGY

Working hypothesis/objectives/model:

Data collection and sources:

RESOURCES AND LIMITATIONS

Location of study:

Equipment and materials required:

Costs: possible expenses:
         amount of time required:

Skills required:

Problems anticipated:

Deadlines:	Presentation requirements
Research completed by	A4 in a single file
1st draft completed by	Summary (50 words); table of contents
Final submission by	1500–2000 words (approx. 8–10 sides A4) excluding diagrams, maps, etc.

ASSESSMENT OF STRATEGY: Decisions reached after consultation:

	Teacher		Student		Comments, e.g.
	Go ahead	Re-draft	Go ahead	Re draft	Suggestions for improvement Suggestions for redrafting
Outline proposal					
Working strategy					
Consideration of resources and limitations					

Extent of student involvement (tick as appropriate)

Initiatives: mostly student's   ..   ..   mostly teacher's

Strategies: mostly student's   ..   ..   mostly teacher's

Figure 6.1   Individual study strategy sheet

The Assessment of Projects and Extended Assignments   77

Another approach to formative assessment, using peer- and self-assessment, can be employed in group projects. This approach is particularly appropriate in top primary and lower secondary classes. Take, for example, the class of 12-year-olds in a Scottish school who were engaged in a comparison between their own community and a community in India. The teacher's objectives are shown in Figure 6.2. Pupils were divided into three groups, and set the tasks outlined at the foot of the figure. In addition, each pupil kept a progress record (Figure 6.3). The teacher might have attempted to keep a detailed assessment of each pupil's attainments in a number of areas (e.g. ability to define the problem, selection of evidence, field work, study and assessment of evidence, conclusions and objectivity). This, however, is a daunting task. An alternative is to discuss with the class the kinds of skills they are acquiring through this kind of study, and ask each group, and each individual, to use the following profile:

NAME:	Very good	Good	Fair	Poor
Inquiry skills (finding out facts)	....	....	....	....
Interpreting skills (finding meaning)	....	....	....	....
Communication skills (asking, explaining, listening)	....	....	....	....
Writing	....	....	....	....
Making maps, diagrams, drawings	....	....	....	....
Comments:				

Each individual assesses himself, and also uses the assessments of others in his/her group to evaluate his or her contribution to the group's work.

This kind of assessment should lead to discussion on inquiry skills, interpretation and communication, and how these can be improved. It should *not* lead to ranking of pupils: peer-assessment and self-assessment are extremely valuable formatively, but are sensitive areas. They can only be learned through practice in a learning environment that fosters openness, trust and honesty, not rivalry.

Comparison of a Local Community (Craigmillar) with a Community in India (Karamsad)

General aims	Concepts	Skills	Content	Methods
1. To encourage pupils to examine evidence and to reach conclusions based on evidence.	Pupils will understand: a. that there are different cultures,	Pupils will be able to: 1. Examine and interpret source material.	NUTRITION IN TWO COMMUNITIES. THEIR OWN AND KARAMSAD.	Pupils, in groups, will apply themselves to a problem concerning nutrition.
2. To help pupils develop problem-solving skills.	b. that these cultures have different values and beliefs,	2. Interpret maps, charts and other statistical evidence.		a. In their own community. b. In Karamsad.
3. To increase pupils understanding of different cultures.	c. that these differences manifest themselves in a variety of ways,	3. Prepare structured questionnaires and conduct interviews.		After comparing the two communities they will prepare a written report.
4. To show the relationship between income, culture and nutrition in two communities.	d. that any one culture is as valid as another.	4. Solve a problem using the above skills (i.e. arrive at an objective conclusion).		
5. To encourage pupils to develop attitudes of objectivity and concern for others.		5. Practise the skills of analysis and synthesis in order to produce a written report		

Group 1
Problem/Task

1. Find out how much people spend on food (as proportion of income) a. in Craigmillar, b. in Karamsad.
2. On what other things apart from food do people in both communities spend their wages?
3. What are the differences between the two places?

Group 2
Problem/Task

1. What types of food to people eat a. in Craigmillar, b. in Karamsad?
2. What is the nutritional value of these foods?
3. What are the differences?

Group 3
Problem/Task

1. Find out the different types of shops to be found in a. Craigmillar, b. Karamsad.
2. Find out the different ways food is packaged in the two communities.
3. What are the differences?

Figure 6.2   Comparison of Craigmillar (Scotland) and Karamsad (India)

79

Two Communities – Craigmillar and Karamsad

Pupil's Progress   *Name*

Problem	Craigmillar	Karamsad
1. Make a list of all the evidence you have studied (slides, films, books, notes, documents, questionnaires).		
2. What did each piece of evidence tell you? e.g. What did you learn from a slide?		
3. Did you carry out an interview?		
4. On the basis of your evidence what conclusion did you reach?		
5. What differences did you find between the two communities?		
6. Do you think either community has a problem which needs to be tackled?		

Source: D. McKenzie, Castlebrae High School, Edinburgh.

Figure 6.3   Two communities: Craigmillar (Scotland) and Karamsad (India)

Performance Assessment

A rather different approach, suitable for use with older pupils, submitting individual projects, is assessment based on performance.

The pupil needs to know how his or her work will be assessed. As this is often based on a final report, guidelines should be given about presentation. Figure 6.4 is an example based on Modern Studies, but with a few adaptions it could be used in many other subject areas, from Religious Studies to Biology, from English to parts of the Home Economics syllabus.

Figure 6.5 shows a more detailed assessment scheme which could be used in conjunction with guidelines for presentation. (Here a slightly different presentation is implied, including a summary, table of contents, and so on.) Scoring is relatively simple and fast. It is the weighting of the marks – how much each raw score is multiplied by – that gives flexibility to such a mark scheme. For example, field work might be particularly important in, say, a project on environmental pollution or consumer education: it could be multiplied by 4 or 5. In an English project on, say, animals as a theme, more weight would clearly be attached to creative writing or wide and deep reading. It is just as well to include a rather broad category ('critical thinking', 'problem-solving' or 'creativity', for example) to give weight to qualities that you find difficult to itemise or specify narrowly, but which you feel are important. The total marks are unlikely to add up to 100, but, using a calculator, can rapidly be changed to a percentage score. If the pupils are to learn anything much about their performance, however, they need to have the marking system explained to them early on in the initial stages of the project. They should also be given the breakdown of their own marks at the end of the project, ideally with oral or written comments.

Assessment Related to Objectives

While performance assessment is based on assessing the pupil's performance on the evidence of the end-product (a project report) and possibly observations of performance (e.g. field work), assessment can also be related to such objectives as inquiry skills, tolerance of ambiguity and so on. Here the assessment may attempt to penetrate below-surface features – how statistical tables are presented, for example – to the quality of thought behind the argument. The long extract (Figure 6.6) is an example of how such objectives can be explained to pupils. Although taken from a technical

The Assessment of Projects and Extended Assignments 81

MODERN STUDIES – 'O' LEVEL – SPECIAL STUDY

WRITING THE REPORT – (PUPILS)

The FINAL REPORT is written on A4 size paper and should be about
1000 words in length, not including reference materials like maps and
diagrams. Write only on ONE side of the paper. Because you have a considerable amount of time to prepare your Special Study the standard of
written English should be high – check spellings, but above all try to
organise your work into paragraphs.

It is vital that the final report is written in your own words because you
should understand everything you have written. Your teacher will ask you
a few questions about your Report to make sure that you know and understand all about its contents.

Here's a guide as to how to lay out your Report. Divide your Report
into 6 sections.

1. INTRODUCTION – This will say why you chose your topic, outlining
   any bias you may have. You should say what you hoped to find out
   and say what you thought, at the start of the Special Study, were the
   possible REASONS and ANSWERS to the problem you were going to
   study.
2. You should now go on to say how you went about GETTING THE
   EVIDENCE, name all your main SOURCES and any difficulties
   encountered.
3. MAIN SECTION – Say what your main FINDINGS were. Cross-
   references (where appropriate) to the APPENDIX should now be made.
   This part of the Report will probably need 3 or 4 subsections of its
   own.
4. CONCLUSION – You have now shown the EXTENT of the problem
   and it's in this final section that you state what the REASONS are for
   the problem you studied and what you think the ANSWERS are.
   DON'T SKIMP on this part of the Report, but remember you must
   present most of your EVIDENCE in part 3.
Sections 3 and 4 should attempt to answer the following 3 questions:
   WHAT is the nature of the problem being studied?
   WHY does the problem happen?
   HOW can the problem be dealt with?
5. A BRIEF LIST OF YOUR SOURCES of information with COMMENTS
   on each source.
6. APPENDIX – This final part of the Report will include examples of
   survey sheets, letters, diagrams, etc.

Source: J. McCartney, St Pius R. C. Secondary School, with G. Jeyes
and K. Duncan.

Figure 6.4   Modern studies – 'O' Grade – special study

FINAL ASSESSMENT OF PROJECT

The final assessment of your project will be made using the following marking scheme.

Score: 3 = excellent; 2 = adequate; 1 = poor; 0 = omitted/totally inadequate

Your scores will be multiplied as shown, so that more marks will be awarded for the more important parts of your project.

	Raw score	Multiply by	Total your mark out of
Summary	3 2 1 0	× 1	/3
Table of contents	3 2 1 0	× 1	/3
Outline of background to study	3 2 1 0	× 2	/6
Main line of argument (hypothesis, objectives)	3 2 1 0	× 5	/15
Evidence/research/observations			
Written	3 2 1 0	× 2	/6
Statistical tables, graphs	3 2 1 0	× 1	/3
Diagrams, maps, photos	3 2 1 0	× 2	/6
Practical fieldwork	3 2 1 0	× 4	/12
Bibliography	3 2 1 0	× 1	/3
Conclusions	3 2 1 0	× 5	/15
Critical thinking: evidence of your ability to reason, to evaluate your results, etc.	3 2 1 0	× 5	/15
Presentation/communication skills			
Report (final draft)	3 2 1 0	× 3	/9
Oral examination	3 2 1 0	× 1	/3

Figure 6.5 Final assessment of project

Fig. 6.6 follows over the next 2 pages

Qualities of a Good Report

A well-written report about a school project should display the following factors as the report is read by a teacher or an examiner.

The planning you carried out:

Your report should show the 'thinking' that has gone into the project with respect to:

a. needed skills – those you already possessed and those you had to learn;
b. available time – how much time was given to the various stages of the project and whether the degree of flexibility you allowed for was reasonable;
c. required resources – how far you made sure the apparatus and consumables you needed were available at the right time.

Your ability to communicate

Your report should include all the written communication which has been undertaken during your project. It should also include diagrams, graphs and drawings to help the reader understand exactly what you proposed to do and/or construct. These should comply with British Standards.

In some cases your report can be accompanied by a spoken introduction, but it should stand on its own, and you may be required to display your project.

A well-organised and well-presented display with clear, simple explanations will demonstrate that you have a good understanding of the project you have undertaken. In industrial circles the display helps when salesmen are trying to influence non-technical audiences.

Your ability to reason

Your report will need to include a survey of previous work. It is essential to record previous developments from which information has been gathered, as well as sources of information, e.g. technical journals.

The sections of your report will need to show a well-structured development of the problem-solving process as well as a capacity to work within limitations; that is, to show a clear understanding of the limitations (available resources, skills and time) imposed on your solution. Your report should also show that you can distinguish between problems for which an answer can be found and those which are too difficult.

The quality of your solution

In discussing the solution you chose, your report should show the following:

a. How your solution matched the specification. It is important here to indicate how far your solution achieved the objectives you originally

set for it, and to note any further modifications that may be
necessary.
b. How you used available resources, time and skills to best effect.
c. The originality of your solution, especially if your solution used techniques and/or design not described in previous works.
d. The difficulty of the problem and how you may have solved a complex problem in a simple way, or gone through some complex thinking to achieve a solution.
e. The potential of your solution for further development or commercial production.

Your ability to evaluate

Your report should show your ability to make:

a. a comparison of your solution against the stated objectives, noting any differences;
b. a comparison of your solution with external requirements, to ensure that outside interested parties are satisfied with the solution, e.g. on safety;
c. an estimate of the cost of your solution and an assessment of the economic viability of the solution.

Differing examination boards describe these five factors in different ways and under different headings. But in general they add up to the same thing and the above guidelines will not lead you astray if you bear them in mind when you write your report, unless you have been specifically told by your teacher to the contrary.

Source: Schools Council Modular Course on Technology: *Problem Solving: Pupil's book* (Edinburgh: Oliver & Boyd, 1982).

Figure 6.6   Qualities of a good report

*   *   *

cont. from page 81

course this explanation could clearly be adapted to projects in many fields – History, Chemistry, Environmental Studies, Fashion and Fabric and so on.

You are unlikely to succeed in devising a satisfactory scheme of assessment for any subject, or any aspect of a subject, unless the objectives are clear. This is particularly important in project and assignment work where the product (the end result that is presented) is probably only as important as the process of getting there: the planning, retrieval, value judgements, problem-solving and so on mentioned earlier.

Most projects containing an element of practical work would include such objectives as the acquisition of:

i.   Skill in observation and recording.
ii. The ability to assess and interpret the results of practical work.

iii. An ability to plan practical procedures and techniques for solving particular problems.
iv. Manipulative skills.
v. Positive attitudes toward practical work.

All are worthy of assessment.

The practical element should be assessed if the skills, etc., demonstrated in it have been established as being important objectives of the course. It is possible, for example in a Physics project, for the practical work to be necessary only to illustrate the theory, an understanding of the latter being the principle aim. In other projects – for example making clothes, serving a meal or producing a play, the practical aspects are crucial to the success of the project. The worst way to assess a project is probably to adopt a style of assessment that is clearly inappropriate to the techniques involved in its presentation.

Biscuits, for example, should have:

* a short crisp texture (obtained by using soft flour, slow baking and storing in an airtight tin);
* regular shape (obtaining by using a very stiff mixture, rolled and cut carefully);
* a good colour (obtained by very slow baking);
* a pleasant flavour (produced by good ingredients used in the correct proportions).

These detailed criteria for practical success are based on appearance, texture and taste, and a pupil's written report is probably irrelevant. For a more demanding project – cooking and serving a three-course meal for a special occasion – the criteria may include the student's demonstration of his or her ability to choose the correct type of food for the occasion, to prepare a well-balanced meal and to serve the food attractively. A check list of criteria may be beneficial.

In some parts of project work the process is more important than the end-product. Figure 6.7, for example, is part of a check list of information-retrieval skills, which could be used to build up a profile of the pupil's skills:

Much more difficult is the assessment of interests, attitudes and values. Here, for example, were some of the objectives for a project on 'people, places and time':

		1	2	3	4

1. Skills involved in the acquisition of information

iv. Asking –

a. devising questions related to a topic

b. compiling a questionnaire

c. conducting an interview/questionnaire

v. Reading and using printed material –

a. locating printed material in a library by use of indexes, catalogues and classification sytems

b. locating information within a single- or multi-volume book by use of index and contents page

c. extracting information from news- papers and magazines

2. Skills involved in the interpretation of information

i. General interpretation skills –

a. select information relevant to the inquiry or study

b. identify the main point(s) made in a source of information

c. classify information

d. identify inconsistencies and differ- ences between two sources of information

e. distinguish fact from fiction

f. distinguish fact from opinion

ii. Diagrams and skills used to interpret them –

a. recognise relationships through simple relationship diagrams, e.g. input–output diagram, flow chart

b. recognise diagrams and miniatures and models of reality

c. differentiate between rough diagram and properly drawn diagram

d. differentiate between plan, elevation and cross-section

e. recognise and use scale

Source: Report of Joint Scottish Committee on Environmental Studies/ Scottish Central Committee on Social Subjects, *Primary/Secondary Liaison in Environmental Studies/Social Subjects*, 1983.

Figure 6.7 Skills involved in the acquisition of information

* curiosity, fostered by the encouragement of questioning;
* wariness of over-commitment to one framework of explanation;
* awareness of possible distortion of facts and omission of evidence;
* openness to the possibility of change in values and attitudes;
* a worth-while and developing interest in the project.

A key to assessing these qualities may lie in the pupil's own self-evaluation. With younger, or less able, youngsters the best approach may be simply to discuss orally with the individual or group the outcomes of the project. How do the pupils respond? 'We could have done better if . . .' is the beginning of self-criticism (though, initially, blame for any shortcomings may be placed on lack of time, resources and so on). This kind of feedback gives the teacher useful information too on his or her skills as a project manager – a difficult role. A more formal use of pupils' self-evaluation is suggested in the following marking scheme, adapted from the Schools Council Modular Course on Technology:

Testing and self-evaluation of the project by the candidate:

a. No evaluation. No testing done of construction work. (0 marks)
b. Poor evaluation with little thought or intelligent comment, or containing unjustified self-congratulation. Little or no testing done. (2 marks)
c. An evaluation with no self-criticism and possible lack of comment about alternatives which, if followed, could have been more profitable (4 marks)
d. A good evaluation including self-criticism where necessary. Possibly suggestions about alternatives which, if followed, could have been more profitable. Some testing done, average presentation of results. (6 marks)
e. A good evaluation including self-criticism where necessary. Detailed reasons given for the success of the project or details given of modifications or alternatives which would ensure a successful conclusion. Good testing done, written up and presented. (8 marks)
f. A successful project with very careful evaluation including detailed self-criticism of the work where necessary. Criticisms of the original brief where necessary and suggestion for future work. Full and detailed testing of the final project done, well written up and presented. (20 marks)

Although intended for a technology course it could apply to experimental work in Science, or field studies in Geography or History, or the cooking and serving of a meal as part of Home Economics.

Problems and Issues

One of the strengths of project work is that it integrates whole areas of learning. A study of local geography - for example, an inquiry into land use of the school site before the school was erected - may lead into many unexpected areas. The old farm on what is now the site of Abbeyfield School may have a history that stretches back to the dissolution of the monastries. Oral tradition may provide memories of old farming methods, seasonal rhymes, earlier industrialisation, the local workhouse. . . . Neither the content (the information) nor the inquiry skills and skills in presenting the information can be compartmentalised into 'Geography', 'History' or 'English', and this can cause a fundamental problem. When we ask a pupil to produce work which is fairly well circumscribed within a subject area it can lead to an 'answer' which is fairly tightly defined. In an integrating activity conclusions may be quite divergent due to the greater degree of freedom associated with project work. Invariably the result is to make possible a longish range of 'acceptable' solutions and this leaves the interpretation of 'acceptable' open. In addition, projects often include creative work, the assessment of which can be highly subjective. Creativity may be in aesthetic areas - such as pleasing design in technology or needlework - but also includes 'creative thinking' and problem-solving in many areas including computer studies, designing experiments in science and problem-solving in technology.

If the project is part of an examination - for example, if it contributes 30 per cent of the marks in a subject where the result can make the difference between admission to a course or rejection - some kind of group marking or panel system is desirable.

A possible routine for this method could be:

a. teachers and assessors list possible areas for assessment;
b. an agreed operation list with weight markings is drawn up;
c. the method of assessing each operational division is agreed;
d. pupils are informed of the assessment expectations;
e. assessors use the methods and weightings to assess projects;
f. assessments are moderated.

A number of other problems and issues emerge in the assessment of projects.

The project is often a group process and it is usually difficult to assess individuals' performances as part of that group. Working in pairs or fours may make assessment easier.

The Assessment of Projects and Extended Assignments 89

Where pupils undertake differing projects the degree of difficulty is never exactly the same, nor is the availability of resources for the project. Comparing pupils' performances is therefore difficult.

Projects frequently involve the community outside the school, particularly in local history studies, Geography field work, opinion surveys, community care projects, and so on. Consideration should be given to ways of including evidence from the community as part of the assessment. Work experience is an example of a type of project where outside assessment (the employer's opinion) may be very valuable. It should also be noted that project work often involves the child's family. This has many excellent results, but it does make assessment more difficult, and disadvantages the child from a poor home background. Again, comparing different pupils' performances may be futile.

Furthermore, there is a large input from the teacher. As part of the learning process, discussion with and guidance from the teacher can be extremely valuable. It is also useful feedback to the teacher about the pupil's approach, progress and attitudes concerning his project. The teacher's notes as planner, consultant and assessor are all interdependent; unlike in other more traditional methods the relationship between teacher and pupil has to be relatively close. The amount of help given, however, should be noted and taken into account in any final assessment. In some projects, of course, the teacher is a legitimate resource along with many other sources of information.

I have argued that certain curricular objectives can only be developed through projects. However, the project may not ensure adequate opportunities for assessment of all the objectives. This is particularly true in group projects, or where the project is short (for example, lasts only a fortnight) or the class large. Under these circumstances only central objectives that can be assessed should be selected for assessment.

Summary

Despite all the problems, project work has much to offer pupils. Both the 'knowledge explosion', and new methods of information retrieval based on new technologies, have major implications for education. Examinations based on the recall of course content test skills (such as the ability to memorise notes which may become less and less useful. Project work, however, develops skills that are likely to be in increasing demand. The skills learned in project work are a far better model for adult learning than the skills learned in examination-orientated courses. The assessment of the processes and products of project work provides pupils with essential feedback on their performance. A well-thought-out approach to assessment can do much to improve pupils' learning strategies and performance not only in projects, but indirectly in other parts of the subject.

PART III

ASSESSMENT STRATEGIES

7
Criterion-Referenced Assessment

The aim of this chapter is to offer guidance to teachers who wish to consider assessment based on criteria, rather than assessment based on norms, as the framework for their teaching.

Norm-Referenced and Criterion-Referenced Assessment

Assessment which is norm-referenced is widely used in schools and in public examinations; thus, although the label 'norm' may sound unfamiliar, it is the most common way of 'sorting out' pupil attainment and is fairly familiar to teachers. Performance is measured against, and relative to, the norms of levels of performance of others in a 'normative' group (e.g. a nation, school, age group, class). Thus norm-referenced assessment is a screening device, separating the sheep from the goats, for finding out who is good, bad or indifferent, by comparing them with others.

Alternatively, criterion-referenced assessment measures performance against criteria. Criteria are previously determined standards which should be passed or mastered in order to pass the test. That is to say, a pupil's performance is described in terms of what he can do (e.g. he can type 40 words per minute without error), rather than in terms of norms or how he compares with others (e.g. he can type faster than Jane or John, but is slower than Chris).

The main characteristics of norm- and criterion-referenced assessment and tests are shown in Figure 7.1.

The same kind of tests (e.g. multi-choice questions) can sometimes be used either as a norm- or criterion-referenced test. For example, you may have taught your class the symbols for chemical elements. You can now test them. If you want to differentiate between pupils you may spring a test on them without warning so that you get the bell-shaped curve shown in Figure 7.2. At the end of term, after a number of different tests, give an

	Norm-referenced Assessment	*Criterion-referenced Assessment*
Frame of reference	Norms, i.e. levels of performance relative to the 'normative' group, e.g. reading level compared with other 7-year-olds; performance in History exam compared with all pupils in 3rd year.	Criteria, i.e. standards of performance relative to course objectives, e.g. 'pupil will be able to respond correctly in French to "Quelle heure est-il?" shown a 24-hour clock'.
Examples	'O' level pass; Placing on sports league; 'Reading Age'; I.Q. Award at Crufts Dog Show; 'Brain of Britain' contest.	Driving test; Certificate as interpreter for simultaneous translator; First Aid Award; Award of University Grant;
Typical educational use or purpose	Selection, grading, ranking, comparison. The emphasis is on differences between pupils and discrimination between them.	To determine standards, e.g. a. minimum competency: has pupil basic knowledge/ skills to cope with next module? b. need for remediation: is pupil coping? (diagnostic testing). c. mastery: has pupil mastered course content? d. attainments: has pupil met course objectives?
Use to institutions, e.g. schools, FE, employers	Particularly useful to selectors, e.g. universities, colleges of FE, employers.	Useful to employers, etc., who need to know pupil's attainments. Also useful in evaluating curriculum, etc.
Selection of test items	Items selected to discriminate between candidates, thus items may increase in difficulty. It is not essential to sample all the syllabus. Examination papers must be unseen before test.	Items selected to measure mastery of specific learning outcomes of course. Pupil is aware of intended learning outcomes (criteria) and may well know what items will appear in test, and what standard he must reach.
How individual pupil can improve	Improvement – moving higher in ranking order at expense of other candidates. A proportion of pupils must fail or be labelled 'below average'.	Improvement – demonstrating mastery of intended learning objectives. It is desirable that *all* pupils master objectives. All pupils can improve.
Method of measurement/ presentation of results	Grades, marks, etc., in rank order, e.g. IQ – 104; History – 65% B 5th in class; 'A' level economics D.	Pass: criteria achieved, or achieved within given limits, e.g. 85% items correct, or task performed within ± 5%.

Figure 7.1   Norm-referenced and criterion-referenced assessments

Assessment: From Principles to Action

A to pupils averaging, say, 80 per cent and B to pupils with 70–80 per cent and so on. This is clearly comparing one pupil's attainment against others. It is being used as a norm-referenced test.

The same test, however, can also be criterion-referenced. You may tell your class that the criterion needed to pass the test is, say, 34 correct items out of 37. 'You either pass it or fail it. Attaining at least 34 marks is the target that you aim for. If so you pass; you "can do", you are competent. If not you fail; you "can't do", you must revise and have another go.' The intention is to produce the kind of result shown in Figure 7.3.

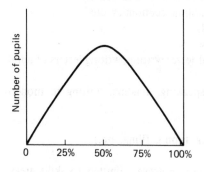

Figure 7.2
Typical distribution of marks in
a norm-referenced test

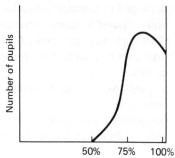

Figure 7.3
Distribution of marks in a criterion-
referenced test, where teaching/
learning has fulfilled objectives

A single example of criterion-referencing, however, does not do this form of assessment justice. It comes into its own especially in skills areas. For example, before joining a sailing course applicants must be able to swim 25 metres. If you can swim 25 metres, you qualify for the course. You have attained the criterion to join the sailing course. If not, you can practise swimming until you reach the standard. Equally, the objective of a course can be stated as criteria: 'At the end of the sailing course you will be able to sail an Optimist class dinghy round a triangular course single-handed on a reservoir in wind force 1–3.' If you meet this criterion, then you have succeeded. If not, you need more tuition or experience in boat-handling.

A criterion-referenced assessment may involve passing a whole group of criteria before passing the test. A real-life example is an MOT test. Here if a vehicle does not pass *all* the criteria (in this case a group of minimum requirements) it fails the MOT test. In a driving test, however, it is some-times possible to botch part of the test and still pass overall.

So the criterion-referenced test can refer to a single item or a group of items. The important point is that the criterion or criteria should be known before the test is taken.

Criterion-referenced assessment ideally has many applications in the skills area. Potential applications of criterion-referenced assessment include assessment of:

- information-retrieval skills (use of reference library, etc.)
- skills used in technical education, home economics, etc.
- skills required in science practicals
- skills required in geography fieldwork
- mastering of punctuation, formal letter writing, writing letters of appli-cations, etc.
- language skills (e.g. listening, speaking, reading, writing in modern languages)
- computer programming
- office skills in business studies (e.g. typing, filing, etc.).

Criterion-referenced assessment is not, however, limited to skills areas: it can be applied in many parts of the curriculum. This approach has proved most successful in mathematics, science and foreign languages, whereas it has been much less successful in subjects or parts of subjects, where creativity, divergent thinking, aesthetic appreciation, empathy and so on are learning objectives.

Using Criterion-Related Assessment in Mastery Learning

Before considering in detail how to construct criterion-related assessments, it is useful to consider how such assessments may be used to structure the teaching–learning approach known as mastery learning.

One model is based on the core-extension method of teaching. Here you structure your materials carefully, selecting the 'core' (key facts, concepts, understandings and skills) to be mastered by all pupils, and pro-viding 'extensions' to which pupils who have mastered the core can pro-gress, while those who have not yet mastered the core have the core-learning reinforced. See Figure 7.4. Materials using this approach are beginning to become generally available, and many existing textbooks can be modified or restructured to enable you to use this strategy.

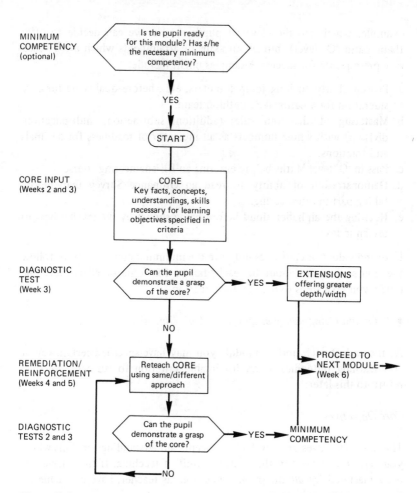

Figure 7.4

Minimum Competency

The idea of minimum competency is straightforward. It may be demanded at the start of the course, or module, or at the end, or both:

● *Minimum Competency as a Threshold*

To benefit from many courses, or learning experiences, there may be irreducible criteria for entry. Here we are talking not about norms (for example, which are the cleverest pupils so that we can decide to offer them Latin 'O' level), but about skills or attainments which are a necessary prerequisite for success. Examples might include:

a. Proven ability to long jump 5 meters, etc., before qualifying for consideration for a national Pentathlon team.
b. Mastering of the four rules (addition, subtraction, multiplication, division) with whole numbers as an indicator of readiness for decimals and fractions.
c. Pass in 'O' level Maths before entering an FE engineering course.
d. Demonstration of ability to read an Ordnance Survey map before taking part in orienteering.
e. Reciting the alphabet aloud before being shown by the teacher how to use an index.

If an individual or class does not have the minimum competency to follow the course you are about to teach, failure for some or all is inevitable unless you take steps to remedy the situation.

● *Minimum Competency as an End-of-Unit Objective*

At the end of each unit or module you may have specified certain key or core-learning outcomes as an irreducible criterion for success. We shall return to this later.

Core Objectives

The core objectives are key facts, concepts, understandings or skills which you regard as central to the course or unit of teaching. If these have not been mastered by *all* the pupils, then you, as teacher, have not achieved the basic course objectives.

Not all aims can be put in stark objective terms and regarded as criteria for the assessment of success. But that does not prevent the teacher from working out for himself and, if possible, also for the pupil, statements about intended learning outcomes for particular teaching units or modules. Figure 7.5 is an example drawn from Secretarial Studies. Right from the start of studying this unit the student knows exactly what he or she needs to be able to do to achieve the course objectives – that is to say, she knows the criteria upon which her work will be assessed.

Learning objectives can be given in even greater detail or more informally. An example of this approach is *Tour de France*, a four-year French course, which uses mastery learning based on criterion-related assessment

An Example from Secretarial Studies
This module is about organisation charts.

By the end of this unit you should be able to read, understand and construct organisational charts. You will be given a test. To pass this you will have to show that:

1. You can state, in a simple phrase, the basic functions of all line charts.
2. Given a vertical organisation chart you can –

   a. state how many levels of management there are;
   b. name the various departments and functions on the chart, and say on what level of management seniority these are placed;
   c. state (in answer to specific questions) the chains of – accountability/ responsibility in the separate parts of the organisation.

3. Given a horizontal chart you can repeat the steps shown above.
4. Starting from a situation you know (e.g. the school, or a local club) you can construct a simple organisational chart.
5. Given a skeleton chart, you can fill in the parts of the organisation from the information supplied.

Figure 7.5   Core objectives

throughout. From the start, pupils are given an understanding of the learning objectives – the 'point' – of each activity. Let me take just one aspect. The 'ability to communicate in French' is a major overall aim. To achieve mastery the pupils are taken through hundreds of 'mini dialogues'. They work in pairs, often role-playing. Obviously, with the whole class working simultaneously it is essential to take a highly structured approach. Each mini dialogue is set up to practise, within a given situation, a couple of language patterns and relevant vocabulary. Here are two examples showing how the instructions for paired work in fact outline the objectives – the point – of each mini dialogue. The first shows the development of language for everyday social use. The Workbook reads:

Parle avec ton partenaire!

One of you is staying with the Garnier family
Thierry or Collete asks you to pass things at table.
You do so, saying, 'Tiens, voila'.
Example: Passe moi la pomme, s'il te plait.
Tiens, voila.

Second, here are objectives for a mini dialogue aimed at developing personal language ('talking about yourself'). The pupil's Workbook contains photographs of pet animals. The instructions read:

Criterion-Referenced Assessment   *101*

Parle avec ton partenaire!

One of you, who is keen on pets, points to each photo and says –
'Here's my . . .'
The other asks what its name and age is.
Then change roles.

Example: Voici mon chien
             Comment s'appelle-t-il?
             Billy.
             Quel age a-t-il?
             Quatre ans.

Narrow though these instructions appear, they nevertheless allow room for
the creative use of language, through role-play and personal language.
Specifying an objective need not cramp development.

The objectives for each mini dialogue are tested during each unit of
work (I will discuss this diagnostic testing in greater detail below) and at
the end of the term in an attainment test. The pupils know the criteria for
success in both the tests. In the attainment test, for example, they know
there are thirty-five 'basic objectives in spoken French'. The item which
relates to the second example (above) reads:

Objective no. 24   Showing photos of pets

                    Target number of phrases or
                    sentences   4

Pupils are told, 'If you can do all these objectives quickly, confidently and
accurately, you have an excellent chance of passing your test at the very
highest level.'

Diagnostic Testing

The simplest explanation of diagnostic testing is that given in Figure 7.6,
again drawn from *Tour de France*. The power of criterion-referenced
assessment is greatly enhanced if pupils know the criteria on which they
are being assessed, and the standard which they must attain. The intention
is that all pupils should be reasonably successful, at least in the core area.

This concept comes as a surprise to many pupils used to normative assessment in which about half the class can be expected to fail. Once they have grasped the idea, it is usually highly motivating.

The term 'diagnostic' is used not in the specialised sense of educational psychologists, concerned with serious learning difficulties. It is used in the simpler sense of diagnosing –

- which pupils are having difficulties
- where and when each pupil is having difficulty
- what are the nature of the problems
- why the pupil is having problems (if possible)
- how the problems can be overcome
- problems with teaching approaches/materials
- problems with learning (class and individual).

A diagnostic test should be based on criteria (learning objectives) known to the pupils. Pupils should also know what score is required to demonstrate mastery of those objectives.

A good diagnostic test will be simple to administer, easy to mark and should give rapid feedback to both teacher and pupil.

Once you have written a good test of a unit you can use it again and again. Item banks of good objective questions are well worth developing for each unit of the course. If carefully thought out, comprehension tests can be used diagnostically. Build them up on a taxonomy, which could become a statement of criteria or intended learning outcomes.

Pupils should be free to take the test as soon as they have mastered each stage. In many classrooms they simply mark the test themselves, using an answer sheet. 'Cheating' makes no sense within this set-up. The pupil knows that the 'quiz' (the criterion-related assessment) is devised to help his learning. Copying answers, whether from friends or the answer sheet, will get him nowhere. He is reassured by the knowledge that, if he finds himself unable to complete the quiz, he will be able to go over the work again, find out his mistakes, remedy weaknesses, and then attempt the same test again. The aim is that he should eventually succeed in passing the test with a high score. Above-average pupils, however, are not held back: once they have demonstrated that they have mastered the core, they can proceed to extensions which go wider, deeper or further than the core.

A well-designed test or quiz should identify which pupils are having problems or are making slow progress, and where they are experiencing difficulties. Discussion with individuals or small groups will often provide evidence on what is the nature of the problem. Some problems are deep-seated and intractable and specialist help may be required: severe percep-

The diagnostic tests

In each of the four Paris topics you will have two diagnostic tests:
a **diagnostic listening test** and a **diagnostic speaking test**.
You take these tests before the end of the topic.

What are they for?
Their purpose is to help you and your teacher **diagnose** any difficulties
that you may be having with the objectives of each topic.

They will help you
They will tell you if you have already mastered the objectives of the topic.
If you **have**, then there will be extra activities for you to do.
If you **have not**, the tests will show you where your difficulties lie, so that
you can do some further practice and then take the test again. This time,
you'll definitely succeed!

They will help your teacher
They will show which objectives have been learnt well by the class as a
whole, and which have not. This will give your teacher the chance to cover
again any areas where there has been general difficulty.
They will show who in the class needs a little more help with the objectives of the topic.
So the diagnostic tests are not exams. They are not for report card purposes. They are something between you and your teacher and are there to
help you.

The diagnostic checksheets

On the next four pages of this workbook you can see the diagnostic check-
sheets.
They show you how you have done in each diagnostic test.
Can you see that you have three chances to pass the **listening test**?
Can you see that you have three chances to pass the **speaking test**?
You will notice that the **pass mark** for each test is very high.
That's because it's important for you to have a thorough knowledge of one
topic before moving on to the next one.

Figure 7.6(a)

Assessment: From Principles to Action

tual problems, major spelling or reading problems and physical problems such as hearing or eyesight, for example. Some long-standing problems are, happily, fairly easily cured. One very bright girl was found to have serious problems with decimals! It turned out that she had missed a vital term at junior school. She had developed her own eccentric system, which had to be unlearned. A short course of instruction was all that was needed. Some problems spring from fairly simple causes: a misheard word, a misunderstanding ('a coalfield is a field where coal grows'). Others may lie outside the classroom: emotional problems, lack of sleep due to late-night videos or early-morning milk rounds. Sometimes the material or teaching method may be inappropriate for a particular group.

Many of the new materials which are currently being developed, build in criterion-referenced assessment. For example, the Kent Mathematics Project, sponsored by the Schools Council, uses the well-tried programmed learning technique. When a pupil is introduced to a new concept, for example, it is presented to him step by step, and he is able to check his responses at each step, so that his difficulties are instantly diagnosed. This type of programmed learning is now being transferred to computers. Computer-assisted diagnostic assessment is also likely to become commonplace. Figures 7.7 (a) and (b) show the use of this in a Science course. After the core of each unit the pupil takes a multi-choice test on the computer (multi-choice tests or Cloze procedure are obvious forms of testing on computers). The great advantage of computers is that they offer instant feedback. Figure 7.7 (a) shows the feedback to the student: note the areas in which he needs to 'ask his teacher what he should do about these'. To the teacher Figure 7.7 (b) is equally interesting: eight questions were correctly answered by all pupils. But what happened with question number 9? Is this in fact a badly phrased question? Or has there been a failure to put across some of the core curriculum?

When a diagnostic test reveals problems the pupil may need to repeat the core unit, or there may be need of remedial materials. Other options are open to the teacher. These include: revising concepts or skills which were, perhaps wrongly, assumed to be known at the start of the course; reviewing or reteaching of the misunderstood part; going over the point again, but with a different approach; rerouting the pupil back to the same point via a simpler level of work, perhaps taking smaller steps at a time; repeating exercises or examples to strengthen the point of weakness; providing a series of simple tests which clarify the type of response required and which enhance motivation through attainable short-term goals.

Unlike some forms of assessment diagnostic testing is not concerned with a final or global mark. Its purpose is to diagnose particular areas of strengths and weaknesses in a pupil's work in order that further work can be attempted or weaknesses can be remedied.

Success in overcoming the pupil's own particular difficulties increases motivation. Breaking out of a cycle of persistent failure is likewise motivating just as constant failure is demotivating.

It is not just another technique of teaching. It is a structured learning process.

Assessment of Attainment based on Criteria

Two approaches can be made to attainment assessment (assessing what pupils can do) within a frame of reference based on learning objectives (criteria).

First, you can build up a profile based on a cumulative series of assessments or tests (continuous assessment). Figure 7.8 is an example of such a profile based on computerised assessment. This kind of technique is likely to become commonplace in the late 1980s. Computers, incidentally, are happier with criterion-related assessment than with norm-related assessment (since the computer finds it much easier to measure success against the learning objective than against a vague 'average' for the year). Note how the pupil has taken a series of diagnostic tests throughout the year: if attainment is the objective there should be a facility for repeating these tests until the pupil reaches the desired standard. Multi-choice questions can be used in tests of knowledge and understanding of 'basic facts and ideas', but this can be combined with a profile covering practical work (this could take the form of a check-list used by the teacher based on observations – see Chapter 9), and with the assessment of 'extended writing'. In this area again the teacher could have learning objectives (see. Chapter 5). The marks or grades given by the teacher can then be fed into the computer.

Thus an attainment test may be built on the foundations of diagnostic assessment and formative assessment. The aim of such a course is that *all* pupils will succeed (whether success is measured in terms of minimum competency, perhaps with a mixed-ability first-year class, or mastery of course content with a group of pupils who will take 'O' level). Attainment tests within a criterion-reference framework will usually produce the spread of marks shown in Figure 7.3; that is, they should all be bunched at the top end, with all, or almost all, pupils getting over, say, 80 per cent.

An alternative approach is to sample, at, say, the end-of-year examination, or end-of-term test, the pupil's attainments at that point in time. For

AN EXAMPLE OF A STUDENT REPORT FROM SCRIBE.
(Note: The total test score 'YOUR SCORE ON THE WHOLE TEST' does
not equal the sum of scores on groups of questions. This is because some
questions were assigned to more than one group of questions, for example,
questions 3, 6 and 9.)

SCRIBE (PRE-RELEASE ON 9.11.81)   STUDENT REPORT

MITCHELL HIGH   SCHOOL REF 1
1EF   CLASS REF: 5

REPORT ON YOUR SCORES IN SECTION 7 TEST

STEPHEN SMITH   REF NO: 14

                                          YOUR SCORE

Conductors   4 out of 6   *
Insulators   3 out of 5
Charges   4 out of 5
Circuits   13 out of 21 *
Safety   5 out of 5
Core questions   29 out of 42 *

Extension A questions   3 out of 6   *
Extension B questions   3 out of 5   *
Extension C questions   3 out of 5

Your score on the whole test 38 out of 60

WRONGLY ANSWERED QUESTIONS

Conductors   3, 6
Insulators   9, 10
Charges   14
Circuits   17, 18, 24, 26, 28, 29, 31, 56
Safety   ALL CORRECT, WELL DONE!
Core questions   3, 6, 9, 10, 14, 17, 18, 24, 26
                        28, 29, 31, 56
Extension A questions   40, 42, 44
Extension B questions   45, 48, 50
Extension C questions   53, 57

**** NOTE TO STUDENTS ****

STARS SHOW THE PARTS OF THE TEST WHERE YOU HAVE LOW
SCORES. ASK YOUR TEACHER WHAT YOU SHOULD DO ABOUT
THESE. IF YOU HAVE GIVEN ANY WRONG ANSWERS, YOU MIGHT
LIKE TO TRY TO ANSWER CORRECTLY NOW. MORE WORK MAY
BE NECESSARY FIRST.

Figure 7.7(a)   An example of a student report from Scribe

AN EXTRACT FROM AN ITEM STATISTICS REPORT
(Note: Only the first 37 questions in the test are shown.)
SCRIBE (PRE-RELEASE) ON 9.11.81 PAGE 1 OF QUESTION
STATISTICS

MITCHELL HIGH	SCHOOL REF: 1
1EF	CLASS REF: 5

QUESTION STATISTICS FOR CLASS 1EF FOR SECTION 7 TEST

QUESTION NO	NUMBER CHOOSING EACH RESPONSE				
	A	B	C	D	E
1	0	0	5	11*	0
2	0	0	10*	5	0
3	4	5	3	1	3
4	12*	2	2	0	0
5	1	0	0	15*	0
6	1	15*	0	0	0
7	0	1	0	15*	0
8	0	0	16*	0	0
9	1	7*	7	1	0
10	2*	7	5	2	0
11	0	0	1	13*	2
12	0	0	15*	1	0
13	0	16*	0	0	0
14	7	1	5*	0	3
15	1	2	0	13*	0
16	3	11*	0	2	0
17	2	12*	2	0	0
18	10*	1	3	2	0
19	0	0	16*	0	0
20	0	0	0	0	16*
21	0	0	0	16*	0
22	14*	1	1	0	0
23	0	0	0	0	16*
24	4	12*	0	0	0
25	0	0	14*	2	0
26	1	11*	1	3	0
27	0	0	0	16*	0
28	12*	1	3	0	0
29	0	3	13*	0	0
30	0	0	0	0	16*
31	13*	1	2	0	0
32	1	1	10*	4	0
33	0	1	2	12*	0
34	1	0	15*	0	0
35	14*	0	0	1	0
36	1	2	0	13*	0
37	1	14*	1	0	0

* Shows correct answer

Source: A. C. Mitchell *et al.*, *School-based Assessment and Reporting Using Microcomputers* (Glasgow College of Technology, 1982).

Figure 7.7(b)   An extract from an item statistics report

An Example of a Profile Report from SCOPE

ATTRIBUTE PROFILES

SCOPE Version 1 on 6/9/82.

MITCHELL HIGH
SCIENCE

SCHOOL REF: 1
CLASS REF: 1

REPORT ON YOUR ACHIEVEMENT IN YOUR SCIENCE COURSE

JANE JAMES   REF NO: 2

KNOWLEDGE OF BASIC FACTS AND IDEAS   MERIT

UNDERSTANDING OF BASIC FACTS AND IDEAS   SATISFACTORY

HANDLING INFORMATION   SATISFACTORY

SOLVING PROBLEMS   SATISFACTORY

PRACTICAL WORK   MERIT

EXTENDED WRITING   UNSATISFACTORY

TEACHER'S COMMENTS:

SCOPE version 1 on 6/9/82   ATTRIBUTE PROFILE

MITCHELL HIGH   SCHOOL REF: 1
1EF   CLASS REF: 8

JANE JAMES   REF NO: 2

A Record of your Scores from some Tests with Questions about

KNOWLEDGE OF BASIC FACTS AND IDEAS

Test	Date Taken	Your Score
LOOKING AT LIVING THINGS	3/11/81	31 out of 38
ENERGY - THE BASIC IDEA	3/12/81	16 out of 29*
A MODEL OF MATTER	7/ 1/82	26 out of 37
SOLVENTS AND SOLUTIONS	16/ 2/82	10 out of 12
CELLS AND REPRODUCTION	9/ 6/82	4 out of 6
ELECTRICITY	19/ 4/82	26 out of 35

Your Total Score is   113 out of 157

**** NOTE TO STUDENTS ****

STARS SHOW THE PARTS OF TESTS WHERE YOU HAVE LOW SCORES.
ASK YOUR TEACHER WHAT YOU SHOULD DO ABOUT THESE.

Source: Mitchel, op. cit., 1982 (see Fig. 7.7).

Fig. 7.8 an example of a profile report from scope

example, *Tour de France* provides for not only a series of diagnostic tests in listening and speaking, but an end-of-year aural and oral test. The pupil knows that there are basic objectives in spoken French: he has been building up to these all year through the mini dialogues. By the end of the first year he should have mastered thirty-five 'objectives' (for example, 'asking for something at table' or 'showing photos of pets'). Each objective has a 'target number of phrases or sentences' – the average is just under ten. (See also Figure 3.2, p. 40.) In the end-of-year attainment test it will scarcely be feasible to test orally the 339 phrases implied in the first year's list. The problem increases year by year so only a sample will be tested. This is sometimes known as 'domain testing' (a domain is a field of knowledge or skill). The validity of 'domain testing' is more open to question than continuous attainment assessment based on a series of tests like that underlying the Science course we have just discussed.

Domain Testing

The problem is, can you validly assess a domain? In a study of History, for example, the area of the domain to be studied could be Roman Britain. Key concepts, such as 'empire', 'conquest' and so on, run through this study. The skill of the teacher/assessor lies in knowing how to identify the key concepts, and how to test them in a way that gives an indication as to whether the whole domain has been mastered.

It may be relatively easy to sample recall of basic facts. It is a great deal less easy to sample the pupil's ability to make extrapolations and generalisations, to understand trends, to interpret data. The comprehension test shown on page   (Figure 5.1, p. 57) provides a model of how an assessment may be made of skills other than recall. But how valid is an attempt to assess higher-order skills and large areas of the curriculum? Each question must in effect be a 'sensor' or 'probe' used to sample a wide area of the curriculum. Furthermore the apparently hierarchical learning nature of some subjects – for example, foreign languages and mathematics – means that it is not sufficient to choose randomly in order to assess the whole domain. If knowledge has to be accumulated in a certain order, particular care must be taken in assessing each step of the hierarchical learning.

Valid domain-referenced testing, it is argued by proponents, is a matter of sampling – of selecting test items that are a valid sample so that an accurate estimate of the pupil's mastery of the domain as a whole can be obtained. It is often difficult, however, to write tests which are true and unbiased samples of the domain and still of practicable length.

Other Approaches

Profiles

In some forms of grid profiling a list of descriptors can be labelled as
'criteria'. Profiles can be used as a check-list to assess parts of the course;
for example, as a format for recording teacher-observations of project work
or science practicals, performance in spoken language or, indeed, extended
written responses (see Chapter 5). A profile can be also used to record
personal and work skills: see Figure 7.9.

If the main use of these descriptors is to establish what can or cannot
be done they can accurately be described as criterion-referenced descriptors – or attainments.

If, however, they are to be used for comparing different pupils' attainments, they are being used as a norm-referenced form of assessment. In
some recent profiles where grid criteria are used there is an added compli-
cation and although grids are not labelled as grades, certification based
upon the grid leads to the profile being used in a norm-referenced way,
with pupils being give a grade.

Profiles are further discussed in Chapter 9, where some of the problems
and defects of this type of profile are examined.

Individual Learning Objectives

Usually the intended learning outcomes – the objectives – are set by the
teacher or other decision-makers in the educational system. The possibility
that students themselves can have their own learning goals should not,
however, be overlooked. This is the idea which lies behind 'contract
learning' or 'trainee-centred reviewing'. Basic to this approach is the setting
of goals. I want to learn enough German to go on an exchange holiday, the
student decides (or: I want to improve my spelling/build a working model
of a hovercraft/learn to service my own motor-bike/play the guitar/prove I
can look after mentally handicapped children/programme a computer/
understand fractions). For some of these learning programmes the criteria
for success are clear: either you have, or you have not, succeeded in
building a working model of a hovercraft. For some the criteria may be
very personal (proving to yourself that you can look after mentally handicapped children). But for many students a series of personal learning
objectives can be very helpful. These criteria can be worked out in discussion with the tutor. For example, the student with a spelling problem may
set out to reduce the number of errors from, say, an average of one word

Category	Grade 1	Grade 2	Grade 3	Grade 4
Graphs and tables	can read simple tables, including timetables with 24 hr clock.	can read straight line graphs and bar charts and use simple conversion tables. ✓	can read and construct a variety of graphs from tables of figures. ✓	can interpret complex graphs and select type most suitable for purpose. ✓
Visual understanding and expression	can interpret simple visual displays such as roadsigns or outline maps.	can produce simple 2-D sketch maps or diagrams, and interpret symbols on them. ✓	can give a clear explanation by sketches and diagrams, can interpret scales. ✓	can communicate complex visual concepts adeptly and appropriately. Some ability to design.
Dexterity and co-ordination	can use simple tools. Sometimes clumsy, not unsafe.	can reliably perform basic manipulative tasks. ✓	can use every-day hand and power equipment safely and efficiently. ✓	can use a variety of tools with stamina and skill, producing good quality results. ✓
Problem-solving	can reliably follow routine procedures only with guidance.	can tackle simple problems such as fault-finding by following standard procedures. ✓	can plan events (such as a meeting), select alternative solutions to given problems. ✓	can independently derive, implement and evaluate solutions to a variety of types of problems.
Every-day coping skills	can achieve basic tasks, such as making tea, under supervision.	can undertake simple every-day tasks such as using taps and can operate some domestic equipment, such as a washing-machine. ✓	can undertake a range of tasks, use and maintain every-day machinery. ✓	self-reliant, could fend for him/herself, even in unfamiliar surroundings.
Learning skills	can learn in a limited range of contexts, with help.	familiar with basic techniques, needs help with planning. ✓	can use most standard techniques, and select appropriate ones. ✓	can learn effectively by a variety of means and can plan own learning strategies.

General interpretations of Grades   The criteria described above indicate that:
Grade 1   means that the student shows both a good level of skill and the ability to deploy it appropriately.
Grade 4   signifies a very basic level of skill, and that the student probably needs frequent supervision during its use.

Source: Profiles (Further Education Curriculum Review and Development Unit, 1982).

Figure 7.9   Part of profile

in three to 1:20. It will be helpful if he sets himself a series of attainable intermediate objectives, such as, for example, working through three cards daily from *Blackwell's Spelling Workshop*, and taking a weekly test to discover if he is mastering the workshop's contents. Norm-related assessment offers little information or support to either the poor speller or the computer whiz-kid, while criterion-related (self-) assessment may enable these youngsters to monitor their progress.

Constructing and Using Criterion-Referenced Tests

If you decide to move from norm-referencing assessment to assessment procedures based on learning objectives and using criterion-referencing, you will obviously need to restructure the teaching/learning in your classroom. This need not be completely drastic: the objectives stated in the module on organisation charts (Figure 7.5, p. 101) are just the same as those curricular aims which were previously being employed in this business studies course. The difference lies in the context in which the test is used, the purpose in administering it and the nature of the follow up.

Suppose you are constructing, or revising, a simple classroom test. (Tests used on a wider scale require pre-testing, evaluation and standardisation at a level of sophistication not dealt with here.) There are three steps in constructing a test.

1. *Specify the Behaviour you Expect*

A criterion-referenced test should tell us what relevant tasks the pupil can perform which demonstrate mastery or competency. Such tests, therefore, are based upon a careful analysis of which tasks best demonstrate this, and a clear pre-specification of these behaviours. These are often written in terms of behavioural objectives, e.g. using long-division techniques, the pupil will be able to calculate whole-number sums correctly. The objectives of the unit on organisational charts (Figure 7.5) and the objectives for the mini dialogues in *Tour de France* are further examples.

It is not only the teacher and the test constructor who needs to have a clear idea of what these behaviours are, but the learner also. In many cases the pupil knows, from the start of the course, almost the exact nature of the test that will come at the end. The aim is mastery and competency and if all the pupils attain this so much the better. Surprise questions and 'unseen' papers are a device for attaining the bell-shaped curve shown in Figure 7.2, rather than the one shown in Figure 7.3, with all pupils obtaining, say, 75 per cent or more.

In writing behavioural objectives (that is, the criteria for a criterion-referenced test) the following guidelines might be useful:

i. Be as precise as possible about exactly what you want the pupil to be able to do – avoid vague words such as 'understand', 'know', 'appreciate'.

ii. Use specific words that indicate how the pupil will demonstrate in observable form that he has achieved the objective: instead of 'the pupil will have a knowledge of the Liverpool Football Club', you should specify behaviours such as 'the pupil will be able to name ten well-known players'.

iii. There should be some indication of the degree or level of performance expected: for example, 'the pupil will be able to name, in writing, using correct spelling, at least ten famous players, and be able to say briefly why they are famous'.

iv. You should be clear about the conditions under which these objectives are met: for example, the time limit set for the task, what information or apparatus are provided, whether group co-operation is allowed and so on. Where necessary these should be stated on the test.

2. Determine the Level of Competence you Expect

As well as assuming pre-specified behaviour, you need a previously determined level of competence in criterion-referenced tests.

At what level should the required standard of performance be set? Do you need 100 per cent mastery? Is 80 per cent of the items correct good enough? Is a 10 per cent margin of error acceptable?

There are several factors which might be taken into account. First, what is the purpose of the test? Is the test for minimum competency, perhaps set at a deliberately low level to encourage or motivate slow learners? Or is the aim that all pupils should master a more demanding course?

When criterion-referenced testing involves laying down absolute standards for attainment careful consideration must be given to what they are. For instance, do they sample the domain adequately? Is it necessary to pass all the questions in order to assess whether or not a person passes the test overall? A degree of inadequacy in sampling or attainment may, for example, be acceptable in English if one knows that similar topics will be covered later on. That may be unacceptable in Mathematics where mastery of one form of knowledge is essential before one can progress further.

What is considered as adequate evidence of 'competency' and 'mastery' depends upon –

a. past experience of what levels of skill or knowledge have proved adequate for a task to be performed efficiently or safely; or have proved an adequate base for some other operation or learning experience. For example, how much Maths do you need for 'A' level Physics? How much French do you need to know to correspond with a penfriend? How much knowledge of Anatomy do you need to examine a patient if you are a GP?

b. Established standards – these, of course, can change or differ from one place to another. The qualifying standards for the Olympic Games have risen considerably in the last fifty years. The criterion for minimum competency in Latin is probably less severe now than when Classics dominated the school curriculum.

c. The nature of the task itself – a driver must be able to operate his brakes or a pilot to land his aircraft with 100 per cent competency, 90 per cent will not do. On the other hand, total recall and a profound understanding of all the causes of the First World War may not be necessary or even possible at 'A' level.

The 'cut-off' point is not always a matter of the global score achieved in the test. Sometimes it is a matter of the nature, relevance and difficulty of the different items which make up the test. In some tests a useful procedure is to arrange the items in groups according to the level of mastery required. For example, after a few lessons on map reading and the interpretation of maps, a test or quiz might be given. In Part I (identifying basic symbols, e.g. roads, rivers, railways and towns), the pupil must answer all the items correctly; in Part II (taking bearings from A to B) an acceptable standard might be 80 per cent accuracy; in Part III, where perhaps understanding of process – say, drawing a plan of the school – might be more important than the accuracy of correctness of the end-product, 30 per cent might be sufficient evidence that the process has been understood even if it cannot yet be applied.

3. *Select the Test Items*

To be included in a test, items must satisfy three points:
(a) They must be very closely related to the pre-specified behaviours or objectives.

(b) They must reflect the previously determined level of competency. The aim is to determine whether or not this standard has been reached, and not to ask easy or difficult questions in order to achieve a spread of marks.

(c) They must be valid samples of the domain that is being tested.

Several questions (or parts to a question) must be selected to test any objective unless it is extremely simple. One item on its own would not be a valid assessment.

Provided these points are met the actual form that the item takes may not be very different from a norm-referenced test. Techniques are discussed in Chapters 4 to 6.

Problems and Advantages of Criterion-referenced Testing

Many of the well-rehearsed arguments against using behavioural objectives apply also to the use of criterion-referenced test. Writing tests may be extremely time-consuming, and the fundamental restructuring of teaching/ learning makes considerate demands on teachers, although, with the intro- duction of more materials based on mastery learning, this will become less daunting.

In actually writing a test a high degree of precision (involving clear iden- tification of objectives, the standard to be attained and the conditional requirements for the test) is often required in deciding the level or criterion that is acceptable. Numerous questions may be necessary to ensure reliable testing of each key element of knowledge/skill/understanding. You will need some proficiency in deciding which questions are, in fact, the best discriminators for this purpose.

Even so, criterion-referenced tests may measure only short-term objec- tives; their use requires a level of pre-planning and inflexibility in the curriculum and assessment scheme that may be undesirable. Finally, it is difficult to assess high-order objectives with them and as Ebel says – 'Knowledge does not come in discrete chunks that can be defined and identified separately.'

Does this mean that the concept of using a criterion-referenced frame- work is out of the question for the practising teacher?

Classroom experience shows that, once pupils understand the new approach, criterion-referencing is not only acceptable but motivating. Not everything needs to be tested in a formal, examination-like setting. Often pupils experienced in using objectives mark their work, using an answer sheet. Marking criterion-referenced assessments may, in fact, make far fewer demands on the teacher's time compared with marking norm-referenced assessments. However, after pupils have marked their work they then consult their teacher about whether they need more back-up work on the core to master key content and skills, or are ready for extension work. This can be demanding.

If you return to the examples in Figure 7.5 (the example from secretarial studies, p. 101) you will see that testing the pupils' success is often no more difficult within a criterion-referenced framework than it would be within a norm-referenced framework. The same test could be used. *It is the context in which tests are used and the purpose in administering them, and the nature of the follow-up, which is different.*

Describing the Results of the Test

For criterion-referenced purposes the results of a test are usually given in the form of a statement of what the pupil has shown he can do. Figure 7.8 - the example of a profile report in a Science course - is a good example. By contrast a norm-referenced test is more likely to state the results of an overall percentage, or an order of merit, or a grade, without describing what the pupil has actually demonstrated he can do, or suggesting areas for improvement.

It is, as Ebel observes in *Essentials of Educational Measurement* (1972), excel is more important than knowing what he can do. However, the difficulty of conveying to pupils and their parents the difference between norm-referenced assessment and criterion-referenced assessment should not be underestimated: in criterion-referenced assessments almost all pupils should succeed and parents (and pupils) may interpret an 80 per cent mark as eveidence that their child is well above average in ability, rather than evidence that s/he has mastered foundation science.

Conclusion

Norm-referenced assessment and criterion-referenced assessment are alternative, sometimes complementary, approaches. Both have strengths and problems. This should be taken as a reminder that fitness for purpose is a key concept in assessment, and that no single mode is likely to fulfil all requirements.

Assessment: From Principles to Action

8

Examinations in Schools

The focus of this book is in-school assessment. Much of it has been devoted to the discussion of new and improved techniques of school-based assessment: techniques which should make assessment more valid and more helpful to pupils as well as more relevant to the changing needs of society. However, much of what happens in school is a rehearsal for traditional external examinations. This chapter, therefore, is concerned with examinations in school which are geared to external examinations: with end-of-term examinations, for example, and 'mock' 'O' and 'A' levels.

The Place of Examinations

For over a century public examinations have dominated assessment in schools. Examinations, designed to rank academically gifted pupils destined for universities, have come to determine the curriculum and assessment of the majority of pupils. External examinations are associated with the maintenance of curricular and pedagogical standards. They are widely and favourably regarded as an objective, convenient and credible yardstick of proven worth. Selection for all courses in higher education, and many courses in further education, is based on performance in public examinations, as is selection for professional and technical training, apprentice-ships, and, indeed, selection for many jobs where performance in 'O' levels would appear to have little relevance (see Figure 8.1). The annual publication of every schools' examination results in the local press is further evidence of the importance of examinations as a criterion for a school's or LEA's success (or otherwise).

There is, however, a growing awareness among both teachers and society at large that traditional-type examinations may be a poor indicator of a pupil's skills and abilities.

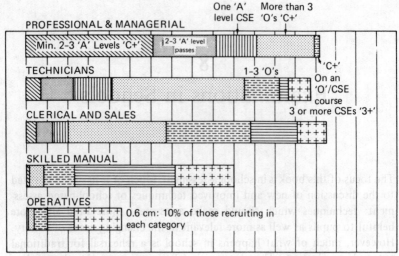

Source: Janet E. M. Jones (BP Research Fellow), *The Use Employers Make of Examination Results and other tests, for selection and employment* (School of Education, University of Reading, 1983). Author now based at Royal Society of Arts, London.

Figure 8.1   Levels of qualification desired by employers

For example, the CBI, in its evidence to the Commons Select Committee on Education and Science and the Arts, stated that 'School examinations are too academic and do not assess qualities highly valued by employers'; the CBI 'strongly supported the development of pupil profiles, recording academic, practical and personal strengths and weaknesses, particularly social and communication skills which conventional examinations are not designed to evaluate'.

This opinion is widely shared and as a result there is pressure on schools to develop a wider approach to assessment. None the less it looks as if the traditional final examination will continue to be a part of many pupils' assessment for many years to come. External certification, whether by GCE, CSE, and SCE or their replacements, may include some form of continuous or internal assessment, but the external, final exam will still dominate assessment for many pupils.

It is not this chapter's intention to discuss further the merits or demerits of examinations (which are considered more fully in Chapter 2), but to look at how teachers can make the best of examinations. That is why this chapter looks at the preparation and marking of those academic examinations, akin to external certificate examinations, examinations which are norm-referenced and are intended to have predictive validity as well as content validity.

Structuring Examinations

Fundamentally the structuring of any exam or similar periodic test should be based on the principles that underly all assessment. Is the exam valid and is it reliable? These concepts have been discussed generally in Chapter 3. Here we will try and apply them to exams. However, it should be said that no exam or test can be completely valid or reliable, and the following suggestions can only help to minimise the factors working against validity and reliability.

Many school examinations are a rehearsal for external examinations. Examination papers are therefore closely modelled on the external examination. While this is essential for training in the 'mock' 'O' levels and 'A' levels, its extension downwards through the school is open to question. Commercially produced papers for the lower school should only be used with extreme caution. They probably do not examine the curriculum you are teaching.

Specification Grids

It is important to be clear about what the aims and objectives of your examination are. To achieve your stated aims you would be well advised to draw up a specification grid.

Ability to be tested	Magnetic effect of a current	Effect of force on a conductor	Electromagnetic induction	Number of questions
Factual recall	4	3	3	10
Understanding	5	6	4	15
Knowledge of laws and principles	1	2	2	5
Total marks	10	11	9	30

Source: Schools Council Examination Bulletin No 32, *Assessment and Testing in the Secondary School*, Evans/Methuen Educational 1975.

Figure 8.2   Test specification for a third-year physics group

Your choice of technique will depend to an important extent on the abilities you plan to assess. Here, for example, is the structure (as opposed to the content) of a local studies examination:

Ability being assessed	Paper 1(a) (short-answer test)	Paper 1(b) (structured questions)	Paper 2 (essay paper)	Practical test (assignments)	Weighting
Knowledge of facts	15 (30 questions)				15
Interpretation of diagrams, maps, tables, etc.		10			10
Application of knowledge, and skills to simple problems, new situations, etc.		15 (4 questions of 5 parts)	20 (2 questions)		35
Ability to make observations, measurements, etc.				10	10
Ability to record results				10	10
Ability to interpret results			10 (1 question)	10 (oral)	20
Weighting	15	25	30	30	100

Source: as for Figure 8.2.

Figure 8.3 Examination specification for a fifth-year local studies course (weightings are given as percentages)

Down one side are listed the abilities to be examined, while along the top are the type of questions to be used and the weighting to be attached to these.

To select the techniques most appropriate to your plans remember the concept of fitness for purpose. There should be variety and balance, reflecting the different skills which are being assessed and the different teaching/learning situations pupils have experienced.

Choice of Techniques: Validity and Reliability

Short-answer questions, structured questions and comprehension tests. Short-answer questions, such as multi-choice questions, are probably the most valid method of sampling factual recall widely if superficially. These have been discussed in Chapter 4 on Objective Tests.

Structured Questions (discussed in Chapter 5) are also a valid method of sampling recall.

For the exam setter, writing objective tests is probably more demanding than writing structured questions, but the marking of objective tests is easier. A 'bank' of well-written items should be built up in the department for use in examinations.

Both these techniques have a relatively high reliability, in that candidates would probably produce much the same sort of results in a repeat of a very similar examination, and fairly reliable comparisons can be made between candidates. Their predictive reliability is only fair in that, if a candidate does reasonably well in, say, multi-choice questions in a second-year examination, there is a fair chance that she will perform reasonably well in a similar test at 'O' level – provided (and this is extremely important), she still likes her teachers and the subject. The predictive value in other respects is probably poor. An 'A' level pupil who does extremely well in the multi-choice section in, say, Chemistry will not necessarily be able to handle the problem-solving, laboratory work and reasoning required in advanced courses at university.

Ideally, examinations should also test higher-order cognitive skills; the ability to understand concepts, to apply knowledge to new situations, to make inferences, to analyse trends, to evaluate information, to generate solutions. To a limited extent a very well-designed comprehension exercise can test this, though over-training in 'comprehension' is stultifying. Nevertheless, a comprehension exercise can be a highly sensitive tool, capable of testing higher cognitive skills if carefully planned with this in mind.

Extended writing (see Chapter 5) is the most obvious choice for the valid assessment in examinations of higher cognitive skills. However, some research has shown that many exam essay questions demand only recall rather than the application of concepts and understandings, evaluation and synthesis. In a Schools Council Research Study, Biology questions were rated by an experienced panel to see which cognitive skills were being assessed. Two typical Biology questions were analysed. The first read:

Describe, with the aid of a labelled *diagram*, a named fish and *outline* its life-history. *Explain* how it moves and breathes.

Here, in the opinion of the panel, the key words, "describe", "diagram" and "outline" were concerned almost entirely with factual knowledge, while "explain" required some comprehension in addition. The application of analysis and evaluation were both untested.

A second question read:

> For Christmas, Sian was given a puppy, 'Judy', which was black with white spots. Her sister Gaenor was very envious and she asked for a similar puppy. Her father said that Mr. Hughes had no more, but he would find a mate for Judy and then Gaenor could also have a black-and-white puppy. Some time later Judy was mated and eventually produced seven grey-coloured puppies, much to Gaenor's disappointment.

> *Explain* this genetically and *suggest* the ways you think Gaenor's father might obtain a black-and-white puppy from the animals they now have.

The analysis of this question by the seven panel members was as follows:

Panel member	Explain				Suggest			
	Kn	Com	App	A/E	Kn	Com	App	A/E
1	20	20	60	–	20	20	40	20
2	–	–	100	–	–	100	–	–
3	–	50	50	–	–	25	75	–
4	–	50	50	–	–	–	50	50
5	–	100	–	–	–	100	–	–
6	–	50	50	–	–	–	100	–
7	10	40	50	–	10	10	80	–
TOTALS (average (to nearest whole no.)	30	310	360	–	30	255	345	70
Weight(marks)	9				16			

Overall weighted classification: Kn 4%, Com 39%, App 50%, A/E 6%.

Key to symbols: Kn – Knowledge; Com – Comprehension;
                         App – Application; A/E – Analysis/Evaluation

Source: Schools Council Research Studies:
Alan S. Willmott and Cedric G. W. Hall, *O level Examined*
(London: Macmillan Education, 1975).

Figure 8.4   Panel members' percentage classification of a question from Board 5 'O' level biology (1970)

Further research into examinations by the same research project showed that the emphasis is overwhelmingly on factual knowledge:

Examination subject	Classification (%)			
	Kn	Com	App	A/E
Board 1 biology (1970)	62	27	11	1
Board 1 biology (1971)	66	22	10	2
Board 2 biology (1970)	55	23	15	7
Board 5 biology (1970)	55	36	8	1
Board 5 physics (1971)	54	36	9	1
Board 7 geography (1970†	54	29	8	8
Board 7 geography (1971)†	60	29	6	4

* For key to symbols, see Table 8.3
† Based on only a selection of questions.

Figure 8.5   Overall classification of seven 'O' level examinations according to the modified Bloom, Taxonomy

A worrying finding in this study was that good candidates who choose to do more demanding questions (requiring the application of knowledge and concepts, and analysis and evaluation) are severely disadvantaged. The marking system ensures that it is easier to score highly on purely factual questions. One of the reasons for the success of crammers is that they train pupils both to spot the 'easy' questions, requiring simple factual recall, and to memorise factual information in the shape of standard model answers. Candidates are taught the trick of adapting the opening sentence or paragraph to produce a relevant answer to a standard question. They are advised to steer clear of difficult, challenging questions.

The element of luck plays so important a part in the success, or otherwise, of candidates that essays are very unreliable. As with many techniques, the essay is fairly reliable in predictive terms for the exceptionally able pupil, who can produce a good-to-excellent essay on most topics, and for the very poor pupil, who will fail in every topic. The unreliability of middle-ranking pupils' essays is notorious.

Alternative approaches: open-book examinations and 'take aways' One way of improving the validity and reliability of essays and extended writing is to set 'open-book' examinations. For example, candidates faced with a French translation or essay are allowed to take in dictionaries and grammar books. (In unseen translations, candidates who do not know the specialist vocabulary are unduly penalised if they cannot refer to a dictionary. You can also narrow the choice if those taking, say, Biology or History are allowed to take in their own notes, and possibly a textbook. Thus the test becomes not primarily a test of memorisation (although clearly the candidate faced with a question on the causes of the First World War will be unable to organise the material efficiently if he has never studied the topic.) It is a test of the ability to handle familiar sources and information, to reinterpret it, and to analyse and synthesise.

Examinations concerned mainly with the recall of information are often organised as tests of speed – working against the clock. Examinations intended to assess higher cognitive skills are more sensibly designed as power-tests. Hence the *'take away'*, where an essay subject is set (no choice is allowed), and the candidates, with this advance warning, have a few days, or even a month, in which to research, plan and write their answers. This approach is quite widely used in universities, but also works with boys and girls on foundation courses, where the test may not take the form of an essay, but a project – for example, researching and arranging a trip to the zoo for physically handicapped children, or filling in application forms, a c.v., planning a route map, or taking part in a mock interview.

The 'take away' allows reliable comparisons to be made between candidates, since they are all doing exactly the same question (a limitation which is impossible in the unseen examinations, since it would load the dice against unlucky candidates who had revised the wrong part of the syllabus). It is, however, a test of skills other than the recall of information (the traditionally examinable cognitive ability). It tests the candidates' ability to organise time and resources, and to consult authorities (both human and resources contained in libraries etc.), in a way much more realistic and adult than the formal examination. It is not 'cheat-proof', though heavy penalties can be given for word-for-word copying. All sources consulted should appear in the 'acknowledgements', and intelligent use of sources should score highly. One aspect that must cause concern is whether the system imposes too great a strain. This can be reduced if the teacher is also a resource, to whom acknowledgement must be made, but who provides support, encourages research, suggest redrafting and checks progress.

To sum up this section on the structuring, setting and preparation of examinations:

* Leave plenty of time for preparation. It takes time and thought to ensure that your exam validly achieves what it sets out to do.
* Be absolutely clear about what are the aims and objectives for your exam.
* Draw up a specification grid for your examination. This should cover both the content of the exam, and the skills or abilities to be assessed.
* Use a variety of techniques – multi-choice questions, structured questions, extended writing, practicals, orals, and so on – to provide balance and to assess a wide range of skills, abilities and attainments.
* Consider carefully the weight you will attach to each part of the examination to ensure that you value equitably all the skills and attainments which are course objectives.
* Take care that there is not a disproportion between the time allowed and the difficulty or length of the answers required.
* Avoid setting trick questions which cover obscure or difficult points.
* Phrase questions clearly and unambiguously, and give clear instructions on how to answer. Figure 8.6 gives a list of standard 'key' words.
* Avoid setting questions which are dependent on an ability to answer an earlier question.
* Use externally produced examinations (e.g. old 'O' level papers or commercially produced ones) only with caution. Check whether they really are examining the curriculum you have been teaching.
* Check the test which you have devised for ambiguities, inappropriate vocabulary, legibility, typing errors. Ask someone else to check it too.

Finally, remember there are two fundamental questions to be asked in preparing an exam. Does the exam validly test the skills and knowledge you have been teaching, using the appropriate forms of questions? Do the pupils understand clearly what they are expected to do?

Preparing Pupils for Examinations

Preparation of pupils for public examinations (and for school examinations which are a rehearsal for public examinations) should include:

* *Guidance and Training in Revision Strategies, including*

Compare	Look for similarities and differences between; perhaps reach a conclusion about which is preferable.
Contrast	Set in opposition in order to bring out differences.
Criticise	Give your judgement about the merit of theories of opinions or about the truth of facts; back your judgement by a discussion of evidence or reasoning involved.
Define	Set down the precise meaning of a word or phrase. In some cases it may be necessary or desirable to examine different possible, or often used, definitions.
Discuss	Investigate or examine by argument; sift and debate; give reasons for and against. Also examine the implications.
Describe	Give a detailed or graphic account of.
Distinguish betweeen *or* **Differentiate**	Look for the differences between.
Evaluate	Make an appraisal of the worth of something, in the light of its truth or usefulness.
Explain	Make plain; interpret and account for; give reasons for.
Illustrate	Make clear and explicit.
Interpret	Often means much the same as *illustrate*.
Justify	Show adequate grounds for decisions or conclusions; answer the main objections likely to be made to them.
Outline	Give the main features, or general principles, of a subject, omitting minor details and emphasising structure and arrangement.
Relate	(a) Narrate — more usual in examinations: (b) Show how things are connected to each other, and to what extent they are alike, or affect each other.
State	Present in a brief, clear form.
Summarise	Give a concise account of the chief points of a matter, omitting details and examples.
Trace	Follow the development of history and a topic from some point of origin.

Source: Roger Lewis, *How to Write Essays*. National Extension College, based on a handout called *Examination technique* from the General Studies Department at Barnet College of Further Education and compiled by A. E. Baker and V. O'Donoghue.

Figure 8.6 Key words used in examination questions

- preparation of realistic revision timetables;
- implementation of revision timetable;
- development of appropriate methods of study and memorisation;
- differentiation between core of syllabus and peripheral topics.

* *Guidance and Training (including Practice) in Sitting Examinations, including*
   - check list of essential equipment to be brought into the examination room (pen, calculator, dictionary, mathematic's instruments, etc.);
   - familiarisation with examination procedures and conditions (e.g. silence, separate desks, no help from supervisor in interpreting questions, etc.);
   - method of attack, e.g.
     how to read a question paper;
     how to answer different types of questions (e.g. multi-choice, structured questions, comprehension, etc.);
     how to interpret essay questions;
     how to plan answers, etc.;
   - importance of timing and pacing, e.g.
     how much time to allow for careful reading of the question paper and selection of options;
     how to work against the clock, using time checks, to complete each section/question on schedule;
     why it is necessary to move on to the next question, even if the previous answer is incomplete, if running short of time;
     how much time to allow for checking paper at end of examination.

* *Guidance on Assessment Criteria*, allocation of marks, marking schemes, weighting, etc., including
   - how marks are allotted for multi-choice questions;
   - how marks are allotted for short-answer questions;
   - what makes a 'good' answer;
   - how to maximise marks.

* *Motivation and Confidence-building*

Good preparation for public examinations involves creating a positive attitude of alert, well-motivated, confident, well-prepared candidates.

Examinations (say the cynics) are a superb method of assessing examinability – and very little else. There is enough truth in this for teachers to give serious thought to improving their pupils' examinability. The obvious way – repeated 'mock' examinations – is not only dispiriting and demotivating, but would be regarded by many as counter-productive and at odds with the basic aims and objectives of education. Experienced teachers with a high success rate in presenting candidates often combine a deep commitment to the education (in the broadest sense) of their students, with a deliberate planned induction of their pupils into the skills required for passing examinations. For example, Figure 8.8 is a guidance sheet drawn up to help 16-year-old students. Most teachers could construct a similar analysis of questions in past papers.

Figure 8.7 follows

Interpreting the Questions

Examination questions have two essential components: i. an indication of the subject matter to be dealt with, and ii. instructions on how it is to be treated. The following notes are concerned with the most frequently used instructions in Higher Grade Modern Studies question papers and how they should be interpreted.

WHAT?   IDENTIFY

What are the main provisions of the Employment Protection Act, 1975? (I,11,b).

Identify Britain's main sources of invisible earnings .... (I,2B,b).

Write a factual answer, but don't just compile a list. Don't number points a., b., c., etc.

WHY?   FOR WHAT REASONS?

Why have Mao Tse-tung's policies been criticised in China since his death? (II,9,a).

In what ways and for what reasons have conditions and opportunities for blacks and other minorities in the United States improved since the 1950s? (II,14,a).

Write about the causes which explain why the prescribed event took place. Elaborate a little on each point but keep the answer relevant.

HOW?   BY WHAT MEANS?   IN WHAT WAYS?

By what means and with what success has the European Community developed better relations with other countries?   (II,6,b).

In what ways have New Towns in Britain been successful..............?   (I,9).

Write a narrative which describes the ways by which the prescribed events were achieved.

Figure 8.7 (cont'd)

Don't confuse HOW? (ways) with WHY? (reasons).

DESCRIBE   GIVE AN ACCOUNT OF

Describe and account for the pattern of support given to the main political parties in the 1979 General Election.   (I,15,b).

Write a descriptive narrative about the prescribed events which has a logical structure and which makes clear the circumstances in which things happened.

Don't confuse GIVE AN ACCOUNT OF (describe) with ACCOUNT FOR (explain). If explanation is also asked for, keep description and explanation separate.

EXPLAIN   ACCOUNT FOR

Explain why Khruschev was removed from the leadership of the USSR in 1964 and account for Brezhnev's subsequent rise to power.   (II,2,a).

Give reasons why the prescribed events took place. State the causes rather than the effects.

HOW FAR?   TO WHAT EXTENT?   HOW SUCCESSFUL?

What aims had the original member countries of the European Community in removing barriers to trade between themselves and to what extent have these aims been achieved?   (II,6,a).

How successful has the United Nations been in maintaining peace between its members?   (II,12B,i).

Compare what has actually happened with some previously identified criterion, statement, aim, etc. It may sometimes first be necessary to state what these criteria, etc., are so that there is something against which to measure the degree of success.

Make the comparisons point by point in the order that they occur in the initial statement. Expect differing degrees of success.

EXAMINE   CRITICALLY ASSESS

Examine the case for and against an expansion in the number of nuclear power stations.   (II,18,a).

Account for West Germany's economic prosperity and critically assess the view that she has achieved political stability.   (II,8A,a).

Write in some detail, making statements, giving arguments and quoting examples for and against the prescribed issue. End with a brief conclusion which summarises and indicates the balance of what has been written.

Figure 8.7 (cont'd)

The use of these terms if often a hint that the opposing arguments are at least as strong as those for. The validity of any introductory argument should be questioned.

DISCUSS   CONSIDER   COMMENT ON

Discuss the aims of the United States and the People's Republic of China in improving their relations in recent years and comment on reaction by other countries to this development.   (II,5,b).
. . . consider the arguments for and against a system of import controls. (I,2B,a).

Write a fairly lengthy discursive answer which covers several aspects of the prescribed issue and which makes statements, gives argments, and quotes examples both for and against. Answers may pose questions which are then qualified and debated. The discussion may be fairly wide ranging provided that it is related to the prescribed issue. Start with a brief statement of the aspects to be considered and end with a succinct conclusion.

Source: W. Jamieson, Modern Studies Dept, Jordanhill College of Education, Glasgow.

Figure 8.7   Guidance sheet for 16-year-old students

Marking

The mark or grade is often the only information available to a pupil, his parents, possible employers, selectors for further education or decision-makers in school. Every effort must be made to ensure that it is as valid and reliable as possible. How can teachers best achieve valid and reliable marking? To start with, a teacher must realise that his standards are never absolutely consistent; like his pupils, external influences such as health and noise will affect standards; the 'halo' effect can mean that a marker may be unconsciously affected by good or bad writing or by his personal feelings towards a child. If a teacher is aware of this, he is already a long way towards objective marking.

However, the best guard against too much subjective marking is to prepare detailed marking schemes. This is best done by preparing exams and marking schemes together. The same specification grids can be used (see Figures 8.2 and 8.3). Ideally, model answers should be prepared and discussed with colleagues – even if you are the solely responsible for the marking. The marking of objective and short-answer questions and even structured questions should pose few problems - though an unexpected answer may necessitate some redrawing of the marking scheme. However, where essay questions are used the marking becomes more complex and subjectivity more likely.

Other, perhaps small, points about marking are probably worth noting. As far as possible, unless fatigue sets in, mark all of one set of questions at a session. Otherwise it is easy for standards to alter. If you do have a break in marking, check back previous scripts to remind yourself of the standard. Likewise when marking is completed, check back scripts at random. It is common for people to mark severely and become progressively more lenient.

Much of school exam marking is likely to be done by a whole department or group of teachers. If this is the case teachers should be aware of all pitfalls facing individual markers, and moreover be aware that a group of teachers are unlikely to have identical standards. To help overcome these variables the following steps can be taken.

First, a marking scheme should be drawn up which all markers are agreed on. If time allows, one person should select ten to twelve scripts, covering a wide range of ability, and mark them according to the agreed marking scheme. The marked scripts should then be circulated and studied before all markers discuss them. At this point it may be necessary to alter the marking scheme. When the marking is completed, again a random selection of scripts should be checked by another marker to see that standards are similar to those agreed. Where scripts are difficult to assess, a second opinion should always be sought. Sometimes multiple marking can overcome apparent discrepancies between teachers. That is, scripts are marked by three people (who do not know the marks that the others are awarding) and the resulting marks are totalled and averaged.

However hard teachers try, they will not all mark the same - even with the best-drawn-up marking scheme. Some will scatter the marks widely, some will bunch: see Figure 8.8. In this example, two teachers were each given 120 scripts to mark. Now, it is often possible to arrange for one teacher to mark all 240 candidates' answers to compulsory Question 1, and her colleague to deal likewise with all the answers to Question 2. But in this case each of the 240 candidates could choose to answer any four out of sixteen essay questions. So the scripts were divided equally between Miss A and Mrs B, with Miss A getting the odd and Mrs B the even numbered papers (the candidates had been seated in alphabetical order). So each marker should have received an equal share of talent.

Clearly, it was not possible simply to use the resulting raw marks, since almost all candidates marked by Mrs B would suffer. One solution is to

	Scripts marked by	
Raw mark	Miss A	Mrs B
80	1	
79		
78	11	
77		
76	1	
75	1	
74	1	
73		
72	111	
71	11	
70	1	
69	111	
68	卌 1	
67	111	
66	11	
65	卌 1	
64	卌 11	
63	1111	11
62	卌 111	1
61	卌 1	1
60	卌 11	11
59	111	卌 1
58	卌 1	1111
57	111	卌
56	卌 1	卌 1111
55	111	卌 11
54	卌 1	卌 1
53	1111	卌 卌 1
52	11	卌 卌 111
51	11	卌 卌 1111
50	111	卌 卌 1
49	1111	卌 卌 11
48		1111
47	11	111
46	11	111
45		111
43		1
42	1	
41		
40	11	
39	11	
38		
37		
36		1
35		
Total	120	120

Note: Each script is shown by one stroke on the tally. For convenience a group of 5 is shown thus: 卌.

Figure 8.8 Tally of marks given by two teachers

Assessment: From Principles to Action

Raw mark	Scripts marked by		Approx % of pupils in each band	Option 1	Option 2
	Miss A	Mrs B			
80	1				
79					
78	11				
77					
76	1				
75	11				
74	1				
73	1				
72	111				
71	11				
70	1				
69	111				
68	卌 1				
67	111	1			
66	11				72
65	卌 1	1			70
64	卌 11	1	TOP 10%	A	68
63	1111	11			66
62	卌 111	1			
61	卌 1	1			
60	卌 11	11			
59	111	卌 1			
58	卌 1	1111	20%	B	64
57	111	卌 1			62
56	卌 1	卌 1111			60
					58
55	111	卌 11			56
54	卌 1	卌 1	20%	C	54
53	1111	卌 卌 1			52
					50
52	11	卌 卌 111			48
51	11	卌 卌 1111	20%	D	46
					44
					42
50	111	卌 卌 1			40
49	1111	卌 卌 11	20%	E	38
					36
					34
48	1	1111			32
47	11	111			
46	1	111			
45	11				30
43		1			
42	1		10%	E	28
40	11		BOTTOM		
39	11				26
38					
37					
36		1			
35					
Total	120	120			

Figure 8.9 Suggested method of grading or scaling

grade the candidates giving the top 10 per cent an A, the next 20 per cent a B and so on (see Figure 8.9, Option 1).

Grades are a method of processing marks so that pupils, parents and others find them acceptable and relatively easy to understand. It is used by examination boards, and for most purposes is as far as teachers need go in processing marks.

If a more precise rank order is required, you can scale the marks (see Option 2 in Figure 8.9). There are mathematical formulae for this, but again a tally is a good working model. Here, 8 'scaled' marks were allotted (rather arbitrarily) to each band of pupils (i.e. 8 marks for the top band, 8 for the next and so on). For simplicity, the scaled marks on Figure 8.9, Option 2, are shown in 2-mark intervals, although obviously 1-mark intervals, or even half-marks, may be needed if a precise rank order is required. The number of scaled marks per band is for you to decide: you may prefer 10 marks for each band, or even 12, giving you a spread from 14 to 82. You will need to compare some scripts – for example, the scripts with the highest marks, and those with the lowest – to establish who should come top, or bottom.

Not unnaturally, the pupil given 80 by Miss A is going to feel aggrieved to get a scaled 72, and the pupil with 67 (Mrs B's top mark) surprised to come top with 73. Explanations will be required about the meaning of marks. It is for this reason that many schools prefer grades to scaled marks.

Follow-up with Pupils

Most norm-referenced examinations results appear in the form of a single numerical mark or grade. This conflated or aggregated mark or grade gives pupils the message that they rank incontrovertibly at a certain point on a recognised norm-related scale, so that they can assume that they are 'better' than some pupils but 'worse' than others, and 'better' at some subjects and 'worse' at others. Yet a conflated mark or grade is essentially inscrutable: in what respect is the pupil 'better' or 'worse' than another pupil? Why has he received this mark, and not perhaps 5 per cent more or less? What are the criteria for making this judgement? Against what scale has he been marked? How can he improve? How can he compare the result in, say, Geography or English with his mark for French or Mathematics? What does his mark *mean*?

I have already stressed, in discussing the preparation of pupils, the importance of giving guidance on assessment criteria. There is no reason why you should not share with pupils specification grids and marking schemes to help them understand why their papers have been marked one way or another. But that is not enough.

The follow-up to any examination needs to be taken further. First, some examinations can be a learning experience, and their assessment used formatively. For example, you can regard taking a 'mock' 'O' level as training in exam-taking, and use the whole experience (preparation for, sitting and follow-up) as a teaching/learning situation. Profiles (see Chapter 9) may be helpful in analysing criteria for success.

Examinations are not, however, simply used in schools as training courses for external examinations. They are often used throughout the school as screening devices, to select pupils for 'O' and 'A' level courses, and so on. As such, they are a decisive influence on pupil choices. Pupils need help in understanding how the marks are used as predictors (as indicators of pupils' suitability for various courses, their employability, their chances of admission to university) and how much reliance to place on marks as predictors. Research has shown that examination success is not a very reliable predictor of success in future employment or in advanced courses. In fact, motivation, interest and commitment show a far higher correlation with success. Nevertheless, pupils often regard exam results as 'hard' evidence of their potential. Particular attention should be given to the often mistaken assumption that marks in one subject mean the same as marks in other subjects. It is often possible for example, to score 95 per cent in, say, Maths, while in other subjects (particularly English) it is exceptional to get over 75 per cent. Yet on such flimsy comparisons, pupils make irrevocable decisions.

Examination results profoundly influence a pupil's life-chances. They affect his choice of options in school. Great importance is attached by pupils, parents, employers and selectors at universities and colleges, to school examination results, and to predictions of external examination results on the basis of performance in school examinations. This lays a heavy responsibility on schools.

Conclusion

In this chapter we have tried to show that even though there is some doubt as to the validity and reliability of traditional examinations, steps can be taken to ensure that they are as valid and reliable as possible. If exams are carefully drawn up, carefully marked and the results presented in a meaningful way to all concerned, then exams will serve their purpose.

It may, however, be useful to analyse your course objectives and decide

	Assessment	
	Examination	Profile
Knowledge of		Profiles can include:
– the facts specific to the area of study	Objective tests Structured questions	Results of objective tests and structured questions
– concepts which give meaning and coherence to those facts	Structured questions	Results of structured questions
– higher-order generalisations linking those concepts	Structured questions essays	Results of structured questions. Extended writing project
Thinking and reflective skills		
For example, the ability to: – interpret experience and data, discerning meaning and order	Difficult, but use of well-designed comprehension exercise possible	
– apply principles in context of study		Obvious area for profiling: see next chapter
– identify and define problems, suggest possible solutions, test hypothesis and appraise evidence critically	Probably impossible under examination conditions	
Attitudes, feelings and sensibilities		
For example, the ability to: – feel empathy (e.g. in English, History, Geography, General Studies, Economics)	Difficulties in exam conditions due to stress and pressure of working against the clock	
– discern and enjoy aesthetic qualities (e.g. in English, Music, Art, but also technical work, History, etc.)		Obvious area for profiling: see next chapter
– be open-minded, ready to examine alternatives and change positions when the evidence warrants it (in Social Subjects, Science, Religious Studies, etc.)	Only possible if exam is very well-designed Open-ended questions indicated	
– be sufficiently confident to learn from, and value, one's own experience		
Social and academic skills		
Including ability to: – work independently	Obvious area	
– work as member of a group	Impossible	
– use source books and study material	Possible ('open-book examinations')	Obvious area for profiling: see next chapter
– express ideas in writing, diagrams, mathematical symbols, etc., clearly and concisely	Obvious area	

Figure 8.10   Course Objectives

which parts of the course are examinable, and which parts are better assessed, perhaps periodically, using other means such as profiling (the subject of (Chapter 9). Figure 8.10 can be adapted to analyse your course. Obviously, whether a course objective is examinable, depends partly on the skill of the examiner in setting and marking. For example, many examinations fail to test higher-order generalisations, not because this is impossible, but because it is easier to set and mark questions testing the recall of facts specific to the area of study. On the other hand, thinking and reflective skills need time, and that is a commodity in short supply under examination conditions, while the articulation of attitudes, feelings and sensibilities may be greatly inhibited in the stressful atmosphere of an examination.

It is to profiles, as a complement or alternative to traditional examinations, that we now turn.

9
Profiling

The idea of profiling has spread widely and seems to offer a sensitive assessment tool, and link up with the move towards continuous assessment as a complement to examinations.

A student profile is a detailed and comprehensive, but usually systematic and open, statement of the pupil's achievements – of his or her competencies and capabilities, and/or knowledge and understanding, and/or skills, learning experiences, aptitudes, personal qualities and maturity. A profile differs therefore from the conventional conflated mark or grade (conflate means 'fused together'): Religious Education, grade C; Physics 81 per cent; French translation, 13/20; Geography field work; 'below average'. The epitome of the conflated grades are GCE results.

In this chapter I will be exploring a number of approaches to profiling, through examples of profiles developed by individual teachers, by school departmental working parties, by school boards of studies and by examination boards.

Profiles are probably (outside education) the most widely used format for assessment. A profiled assessment is essential in most situations where diagnosis and treatment is required (for example, in medicine) or problem-solving is necessary (as in business decisions or in social work). Profiling is also the main assessment technique in most vocational training (for example, in apprenticeships, training of technicians, managers, engineers and so on) and is widely used in career development in major industries, the civil service and so on. The difference in these situations between a record and a profile is not very precise, and there are considerable overlaps. However, it would probably be accepted that while a record is primarily for administrative purposes, and its format is one that suits bureaucratic purposes, a 'profile' is essentially a discussion document designed as a systematic, detailed, comprehensive and purposeful statement intended to focus on, and to assist in the individual's progress and development. As such, the individual often contributes to it, and has access to it; he/she may share in the assessment process, and may be involved in the decision arising out of the assessment – the course of medical treatment, for example, or the career development plan.

Within education profiles are based on differing priorities, purposes and philosophies, such as:

* Profiling for formative assessment, assessment in support of learning to enable students to understand, and build upon, learning experiences – and reflective skills; attitudes, feelings and sensibilities; and social and academic skills) that are not easy to assess by conventional means. (If you refer back to the summary of course objectives at the end of the last chapter, Figure 8.10 you will find a fuller discussion.);
* Profiling for formative assessment (assessment in support of learning to enable students to understand, and build upon, learning experineces – remedying weaknesses, improving performance and optimising strengths;
* Profiling as a means of developing a discussion document, offering more relevant and reliable data on abilities, skills, attainments and attitudes, as a basis for decisions taken by and with the student on curricular, vocational and personal development;
* Profiling as a statement of attainments, including but going beyond examination results, for the use of outside agencies, particularly employers, after the student has left school.

The effect of advocating school-leavers' profiles has been to open up the whole curriculum. Educationalists have been quick to realise that the whole process of assessment of so rich and diverse an experience as education from the age of, say, 11 to 18, with its many and varied outcomes, can no more be packaged in a single, all-purpose, master profile than it can be condensed into a GCE/CSE Certificate. This is true even if it is built up cummulatively over a number of years.

The result has been the development of an extraordinary variety of profiles: classroom, departmental and school reports; checklists, and open-ended comments; comments by teachers, pupils and even parents, and by outside assessors (for example, work experience 'employers'). Profiles may include the results of examinations, tests and observations; they may comment on skills, knowledge, activities, learning experiences and personal characteristics.

Inevitably, this chapter will look at only a few examples of this burgeoning cottage industry, profiling. The examples, many of which are still in the 'piloting' stage, have been chosen not because they are perfect solutions, but because they offer models for further development. In attempting to chart a course through the shifting shoals of these developments, I have been all too aware that we are in a new element. What follows is a discussion of the current position, not an authoritative summary.

Profiling in the Classroom: Formative Assessment

Let us begin where many teachers begin: with profiling as an assessment tool in the classroom, used in the assessment of a particular task or unit of work.

Here, for example, in a 'mini-profile' drawn up by a class of third-year boys for use with a story-writing project. Under guidance they decided on a list of eight criteria for a successful science fiction story, which began –

Short story (science fiction)

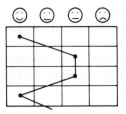

PLOT: Fast-moving, boring, etc.

SCI-FI: Convincing, futuristic

CHARACTERS: Interesting, etc.

OPENING: etc.

This format – a four-point scale (with little faces in the lower school, perhaps) – can be used in a variety of situations: first-year experimental work in science, or a fourth-year community service project; performance in mock job interviews or in an 'A' level translation from German into English; a sixth-former's essay on money supply in economics, or an 11-year-old's talk to the class on her pet dog.

A great advantage of profiling over conventional forms of assessment is that it can be prospective rather than simply retrospective. In prospective assessment the objectives and criteria are open and known at the outset.

This may present an opportunity to discuss with your pupils early in the teaching/learning the criteria for success. You can often 'pull out' of a classroom discussion a profile of what constitutes success in a task. Later pupils can assess one another's work, redraft if necessary and finally produce work of the highest attainable standard. Where the assessment intention is to monitor the mastery of certain skills, understandings or competencies, rather than to rank your pupils, pair-marking or self-marking can be very supportive. It enables pupils to set their own goals, internalise assessment criteria and measure their own progress. Obviously you initiate and participate in the assessment process, but assessment becomes part of teaching/learning, not an extra chore added on at the end of each unit of work.

Profiling offers a powerful formative tool, especially when used in such areas as:

* The development of skills and capabilities including oral skills in foreign languages; skills required in experimental work in science, or in working with computers; practical skills in home economics, technical education, music, pottery and so on.
* The development of writing abilities, particularly extended writing (essays, short stories, dissertations, log books and so on).
* Project work, including (for example) local history projects, geography field work, environmental studies; projects in technical education, computer studies, home economics; community service projects, mini companies (mini co-operative companies), work experience, etc.
* Social and vocational skills courses.
* Courses in which there are curricular objectives which are difficult to mark or grade sensitively, for example, courses which are designed to develop:

Creativity, aesthetic appreciation, imagination; empathy, sensitivity to others; leadership, entrepreneurial skills, co-operative ways of working; political awareness, religious understanding between different faiths and so on.

You will find many examples of this type of profile – a mini-profile relating to a particular task or unit of work – throughout this book. You will probably recall the formative use of such profiles in the section on essay writing (Chapter 5), and the examples given in the chapter on projects (Chapter 6). There are further examples of criteria in the chapter on criterion-referenced assessment (Chapter 7). You will also find in the next few pages profiles that offer models which might be adapted to your purpose.

Profiles and Curriculum: A Departmental Approach

Disquiet with the curriculum – its appropriateness to the learner, its relevance to adult and working life – is leading departments in many schools to question conventional assessment procedures, and to devise new methods, often based on profiles which include learning objectives.

Here, for example, is part of a complex profile worked out by an English department at Elgin High School, for use with first- and second-year pupils.

They began with long discussion, within the department, about the skills areas which should be developed in these years, and arrived at the following list:

Writing .... Imagination and creativity
Ability to write in sentences and
    paragraphs
Basic techniques (conversation,
    letters, newspaper articles, etc.)
Punctuation
Spelling
Handwriting and presentation
Reading .... Understanding short passages
Home reading of novels
Reading aloud
Talking .... Giving a talk
Listening .... Understanding a spoken passage
Talking/listening.. Performance in class discussion

For each skill they developed descriptions of different levels of achievement. Here are the descriptions for 'Ability to Write in sentences and paragraphs', as stated in the reports given to pupils and their parents:

Excellent: Work will show that the pupil has full
control of his writing, using paragraphs
and sentences in a varied and effective
manner.

Good: Work will show a basic knowledge of
sentence and paragraph techniques, but
there will be quite a few mistakes and
sentence variations and paragraphing
will be used less effectively.

Fair: Work will contain many sentence errors
and paragraphs will be ignored or used
inconsistently or incorrectly.

Weak:	Work will be difficult to read because of failure to write in sentences and there will be practically no organisation.
Source:	Jeff Dugdale (Elgin High School), *Teaching English*, vol. 16, no. 3, Summer 1983.

In this example profiling was used as the basis for continuous assessment in the first two years of secondary school, instead of formal examinations. Although it made heavier demands on staff during the year it did away with the tedious marking of hundreds of examination scripts, and provided far more useful feedback to pupils, parents and teachers than the conflated marks of examinations.

From all accounts this profile was both popular and successful. For the staff it represented agreed course objectives, objectives worked out within the department. Attainable learning goals were presented to the pupils: by the end of the two years, as a direct result of the teaching most should have progressed from a weak grasp of how to write a newspaper article, how to deliver a talk and so on to a 'good' or 'excellent' standard. The same would be true of progress in all other skills areas. Clearly, some pupils will make better progress than others. Progress may be uneven. One pupil may have a creative flair but suffer from a serious handicap in spelling; another may have problems with the mechanics of reading. Nevertheless, to both pupils and their parents such a profile offers, in a way that a single mark or grade cannot, an understanding of the complex objectives of an English course, an idea of what are acceptable standards, a helpful analysis of the pupil's present position, and (as the years pass) a record of progress.

My next example is drawn from Science, where a national working party (in this case, drawn from across a number of schools) was devising criteria for a Science course for 14–16-year-olds. They opted for what they termed 'extended grade-related criteria'. That is, they identified certain skills, competencies and understandings as intended learning outcomes of a course in which science was to be presented (to quote from the working party) –

* As a way of approaching and solving many of the problems they (the pupils) will meet in everyday life.
* As useful knowledge about themselves and the world in which they live.

But how, it was asked, do you assess 'problem-solving' (for example)?

The working party offered a cumulative series of graded steps from 6 (lowest) to 1 (highest) up which the pupil can progress. The lowest grade in problem-solving reads:

Grade 6

A pupil awarded this grade will have demonstrated the ability to:

suggest, with guidance, a procedure to solve a given problem

solve a science-based problem involving one operation from additions, subtractions, multiplications and divisions applied in a familiar situation.

Pupils who, in the classroom or laboratory, reach this level of performance are then considered for Grade 5:

Grade 5

In addition a pupil obtaining this grade will have demonstrated the ability to:

suggest an idea that would be a fair experimental test

carry out metric conversion of scientific units.

This assumes that the teacher will set up, throughout the course, a series of learning experiences which provide opportunities for pupils to acquire these skills, and be assessed in them. Some pupils, it would be hoped, would progress fast through this ladder of achievement, reaching, by the end of the course, say, Grade 2, which reads:

Grade 2

In addition a pupil obtaining this grade will have demonstrated ability to:

identify factors which might affect the fairness of a test, introduce appropriate correction measures

solve problems involving at least two operations
calculate percentages.

Source: Scottish Examination Board

Other pupils presumably will not progress as fast, and will end up with a lower grade.

However – and this is where the difficulty arises – some teachers ignored the descriptive profile and reverted to a norm-referenced rank order. This was partly because they were unaccustomed to setting up learning experiences in which the pupil would acquire and demonstrate the required skills as listed in the descriptors. Their evidence of pupils' attainments was therefore incomplete, so they ranked the pupils in relation to one another, and award the 'best' pupils Grades 1 or 2, and the 'worst' 5 or 6.

Problems with Curriculum-led Profiling

This demonstrates some of the confusions arising from the imposition of student profiles without sufficient preparation and consultation.

These problems include:

Objectives and Criteria
In my last example the Science teachers in schools had not been involved in deciding on course objectives and selecting the criteria (descriptors). Unless staff are involved in these decisions, the likelihood is that they will fail to realise the full potential of profiling.

The Meaning of Grades

Confusion arises at a number of levels.

i. Pupils and their parents, and even employers and colleges of FE, are confused by *numerical grades* (1–6, or 4–1). These are unstandardised. In some profiles, 1 is the bottom grade, in others it is the top. Pupils sometimes 'add up the marks' so that a pupil with, say, grades 5, 6, 4, 3, 6 says he has 24/30 and has done better than a pupil with (say) 1, 3, 2, 1, 1, i.e. top grades. *Alphabetical grades* (A, B, C, D, E. F) prevent this confusion.

ii. Less trivial is a confusion of *norm-related* and *criterion-related* grades. Norm-related grades are possible where norms are established. But because profiles seek to assess learning outcomes not assessable by usual methods of assessment (for example, problem-solving skills, creativity, empathy, higher-order thinking skills) it is difficult to 'norm' these. Hence the descriptive criteria so characteristic of many profiles. But some teachers, used to norm-related marks, continue to award, say, a grade C to the 'average' pupil across the board. However, this pupil although moderately good at, say, reproducing the course content in test conditions, may be poor in making inferences or formulating hypotheses, but may have a flair for handling graphics.

iii. Another difference between norm-related and criterion-related grades is the question of *how the pupil can improve* his/her grades. In norm-referenced grades this implies moving up relative to others. Not so in criterion-referenced grades, where the pupil improves his performance (and thus his grades) in terms of the behaviours or performances specified in the descriptors.

Pedagogy and Profiling

Profiling thus challenges traditional norm-related conflated marks because, using a profile, you can

- identify multiple-course objectives which are desirable and attainable, but not necessarily assessable using examinations and tests;
- structure the learning experience to enable the pupil to learn and practice these skills, competencies understandings, and so on;
- structure the course so that you have regular opportunities to observe and record the developing skills, competencies, etc.
- structure the learning experience so that the pupil receives regular and positive feedback through the profiles.

Profile Formats

Formating a profile effectively is crucial is the profile is to be easily used.

You may be able to format profiles in an unpretentious way, and relate the level of attainment to acceptable standards for children of this age (norm-referenced assessment). The profiled report from a Technical Education department (Figure 9.1) does just this. It identifies the skills required (craft and design skills, graphics and work-related skills). It sets standards of achievement. To this it adds space for the teacher's comment on the pupil's progress. Combined, these give a flexible, workman-like, informative profile. A simple, one-page format is all that is required.

| Name of Pupil: | | Class: | |

During S1 and S2 all pupils will follow a course in Technical Education which should develop within every child, not only an interest in Technical Education, but also the confidence and adaptability to enjoy working with tools and materials in practical situations and the recognition of the value of drawing as a means of communication of ideas and information.

To achieve these aims your child should acquire certain basic skills which are continually assessed throughout the course.

The following report indicates how well your child has achieved the basic skills:

Related modules	Plastics	Designing and Making	Combined Craft 1
woodcraft	Drawing 1	Designing for Craft	Combined Craft 2
metalcraft	Drawing 2	Materials	Forces

Skills	Achievement				
Marking out	Proficient	Skilled	Fairly skilled	Has difficulty	
Hand tools	Proficient	Skilled	Fairly skilled	Has difficulty	
Machine tools	Proficient	Skilled	Fairly skilled	Has difficulty	
Design process	Excellent	Very good	Good	Fair	
Solving design problems	Excellent	Very good	Good	Fair	
Understanding forces/mechanisms	Excellent	Very good	Good	Fair	
Recall of tech. knowledge	Excellent	Very good	Good	Fair	
Measurement	Proficient	Skilled	Fairly skilled	Has difficulty	
Freehand sketching	Proficient	Skilled	Fairly skilled	Has difficulty	
Use of drawing instruments	Proficient	Skilled	Fairly skilled	Has difficulty	
Visual understanding	Excellent	Very good	Good	Fair	
Effort	Excellent	Very good	Good	Fair	
Conduct	Excellent	Very good	Good	Fair	
Safe working practice	Very responsible	Responsible	Acceptable	Irresponsible	
Homework	Regular	Fairly regular	Occasionally	Never	

Comments/Progress:

Teacher's signature:

Source: Technical Education Working Party on Assessment, Dunbarton Division.

Figure 9.1 A profile report from a technical education department

A different format is that adopted by a mathematics department, where the chart in Figure 9.2 is used to record the students' success in end of unit tests. Here mastery of course content is the objective.

Greater problems arise with subjects in which the descriptors are complex and detailed because the intended learning outcomes are complex.

NUMERACY PROGRESS CHART

STUDENT'S NAME:..

TUTOR:.. COURSE:......................

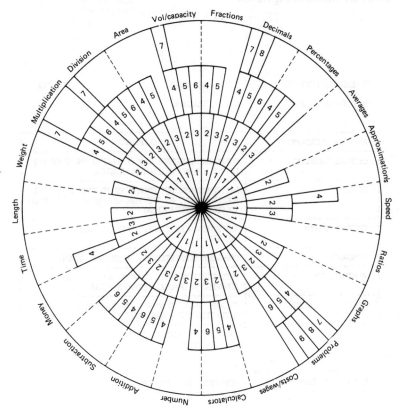

Source: *Profiles*: a review of issues and practice in the use and development of student profiles. Further Education Curriculum Review and Development Unit (1982).

Figure 9.2 A profiled report from a mathematics department

The introduction of computers into profiling is likely to be very helpful here, and will, in addition, greatly ease the tedious chores associated with the administration of profiling.

Here, for example, is a report based on computer-assisted profiling: Figure 9.3.

This page (one of a dozen or so in this first-year pupil's report) relates to his performance in a core-extension social subjects course. The descriptors for the first three categories (overall progress, effort and extension work) are shown in Figure 9.4.

```
 BARR HEAD HIGH SCHOOL               1ST YEAR              DEC '81

    HISTORY/GEOGRAPHY                TEACHER

---------------------------------------------------------------------
I  AREAS OF ASSESSMENT      I            COMMENTS                    I
I---------------------------I---------------------------------------I
I  OVERALL PROGRESS         I PUPIL HAS SUCCESSFULLY COMPLETED THE CORE BUT I
I                           I LITTLE IF ANY EXTENSION MATERIAL       I
I---------------------------I---------------------------------------I
I  EFFORT                   I SATISFACTORY, BUT FROM TIME TO TIME WILL NEED I
I                           I ENCOURAGEMENT BY THE TEACHER; USUALLY RESPONDS I
I                           I TO SUCH ENCOURAGEMENT                  I
I---------------------------I---------------------------------------I
I  EXTENSION WORK           I EXTENSION WORK PARTLY COMPLETED WITH SOME I
I                           I SUCCESS                                I
I---------------------------I---------------------------------------I
I  HOMEWORK                 I HOMEWORK COMPLETED BUT TO MINIMAL STANDARD I
I---------------------------I---------------------------------------I
I  PRESENTATION             I PRESENTATION LEVEL STARTED WELL BUT HAS I
I                           I SUFFERED A GRADUAL DETERIORATION       I
I---------------------------I---------------------------------------I
I  ATTITUDE IN CLASS        I RELATES WELL TO OTHERS IN CLASSROOM    I
I                           I SITUATION AND WORKS WELL               I
I---------------------------I---------------------------------------I
I  ANALYSIS                 I HAS DIFFICULTIES EXTRACTING INFORMATION FROM I
I                           I WRITTEN TEXT                           I
I---------------------------I---------------------------------------I
I  WRITING/SPELLING         I WRITING HAS DETERIORATED               I
I---------------------------I---------------------------------------I
I  CLASSROOM BEHAVIOUR      I BEHAVIOUR SATISFACTORY                 I
I---------------------------I---------------------------------------I
```

Source: Barrhead High School.

Figure 9.3   A computer-assisted profile

4 HISTORY/GEOGRAPHY

CODE	AREAS OF ASSESSMENT	NO.	COMMENTS
A	OVERALL PROGRESS	1	PUPIL HAS SUCCESSFULLY COMPLETED THE CORE AND ALL EXTENSION MATERIAL
		2	PUPIL HAS SUCCESSFULLY COMPLETED THE CORE AND SOME EXTENSION MATERIAL
		3	PUPIL HAS SUCCESSFULLY COMPLETED THE CORE BUT LITTLE, IF ANY, EXTENSION MATERIAL
		4	PUPIL HAS COMPLETED THE CORE WORK SATISFACTORILY
		5	PUPIL HAS NOT COPED WITH MUCH OF THE CORE WORK
		6	PUPIL HAS FAILED TO COMPLETE THE CORE DESPITE REMEDIAL REINFORCEMENT
B	EFFORT	7	ATTENTIVE AND HARD WORKING, WORKS WELL WITHOUT PROMPTING BY TEACHER
		8	SATISFACTORY, BUT FROM TIME TO TIME WILL NEED ENCOURAGEMENT* BY THE TEACHER; USUALLY RESPONDS TO SUCH ENCOURAGEMENT
		9	SATISFACTORY BUT WORKS AT OWN LEVEL AND PACE
		10	REASONABLE BUT NEEDS CONTINUOUS PROMPTING TO MAINTAIN WORK RATE
		11	LACKS APPLICATION, EASILY DISTRACTED
		12	UNSATISFACTORY, LIKELY TO STOP WORKING AND WASTE TIME; THIS ATTITUDE TO WORK IS HINDERING PROGRESS
		13	NOT WORKING EVEN WITH CONTINUAL PROMPTING BY TEACHER
		14	PUPIL IS NOT WORKING TO HIS/HER ABILITY LEVEL
		15	GIVES UP TOO EASILY
C	EXTENSION WORK	16	EXTENSION WORK COMPLETELY SUCCESSFULLY
		17	EXTENSION WORK PARTLY COMPLETED WITH SOME SUCCESS
		18	EXTENSION WORK NOT ATTEMPTED
D	HOMEWORK	19	HOMEWORK COMPLETED SUCCESSFULLY AND NEATLY

Figure 9.4 Descriptors for a profile used in computer-assisted profiling

It is debatable whether a report should contain all the descriptors (as does the Elgin High School profile) or only a selection (as in Figure 9.3). I would argue that it is more important for the pupil and parents to get the kind of detailed, relevant comments of the kind the profile offers than to be able to position the pupil's performance within a continuum of comments. There is also considerable danger in giving so much information – reams of computer printouts – that the recipients are overwhelmed, and lose interest.

The Barrhead profile in Figure 9.3 is an exemplar, not a model. What it does illustrate is the potential in computers for developing sensitive, pertinent descriptors of what are learning objectives in a particular course. It also illustrates, incidentally, some of the clumsiness and syntactical problems of the strange 'telegramese' in which reports are traditionally written. Note the subject-less sentences ('Has difficulties. . .) and uncertainties about tense ('Pupil . . . completed the core . . . ' 'will need encouragement . . . usually responds . . . '). This reflects an ambiguity about audience. Is the profile for school purposes? In that case the use of 'pupil' and the third person is acceptable. Or is the audience the pupil and parent? Would the use of 'you' (e.g. 'You have successfully completed the core . . . ') be more direct and appropriate – and simplify the syntax?

These, however, are minor points. The main point about this use of computers is that the computer can be used to display detailed descriptors (agreed by the whole department as curricular objectives) and even allow for the insertion of individualised comments, while at the same time being highly economical in terms of time and effort, once the program has been set up.

Grid-profiles: An Approach to Assessment of Basic and Work-related Skills

It is not only within subjects that profiling is being tried as a method of developing a more relevant curriculum which will better prepare young people for adult and working life. Often a grid-type profile is adopted to assess cross-curricular objectives, such as the development of communications skills (talking/listening, reading, and writing, calculating and measuring, and visual understanding and graphic skills), and work-related skills.

Assessment: From Principles to Action

Grids appear to be somewhat crude and limiting:

	GRADE LOW 4	3	2	HIGH 1
Reading	can understand simple notices, labels and short notes	can follow straight-forward written instructions and explanations ✓	can understand a variety of forms of writing if simply expressed, e.g. manuals, indexes, business letters ✓	can abstract and inter-pret information (etc.) from a variety of written sources, with-out help
Writing	can write simple notes for self and messages for others	can complete every-day forms and write simple instructions and standard letters ✓	can write clear and accurate reports and compose cor-rect and appropriate non-standard letters ✓	can communicate both information and argument in written form, suiting style to audience and content
Listening/ talking	can carry out simple instructions and can communicate at a conversational level with friends	can follow simple oral explanations, describe straight-forward events, and deal with simple queries from strangers ✓	can make a clear and accurate oral report, interpret more com-plex instruction and be effective on the telephone and at interview ✓	adept at most kinds of verbal encounter, e.g. group discussion, making and dealing with com-plaints, public speaking
Calculations	can do simple whole number calculations using 4 arithmetic rules	can do simple calcu-lations by mental arithmetic and con-vert fractions to decimals and per-centages for every-day purposes, e.g. money ✓	can use simple for-mulae substitutions, and ratio. Accurate with every-day calcu-lations ✓	quick and accurate at complex calculations and problems in a variety of contexts

LOW .... _HIGH_

Problem-solving	can reliably follow routine procedures only with guidance	can tackle simple problems such as fault-finding by following standard procedures ✓	can plan events (such as a meeting) select alternative solutions to given problems ✓	can independently derive implement and evaluate solutions to a variety of types of problems
Every-day coping skills	can achieve basic tasks such as making tea, under super-vision	can undertake simple every-day tasks such as using taps and can operate some domestic equipment-such as a washing-machine ✓	can undertake a range of tasks, use and maintain every-day machinery ✓	self-reliant, could fend for him/herself, even in unfamiliar surroundings
Learning skills	can learn in a limited range of contexts, with help	familiar with basic techniques, needs help with planning ✓	can use most standard techniques, and select appropriate ones ✓	can learn effectively by a variety of means and can plan own learning strategies

Source: _Profiles_, Further Education Curriculum Review and Development Unit

Figure 9.5 A grid-type profile

There are a number of major problems in this type of grid-profile. These include:

* Audience: for whom is the profile intended – the student? parents? employers?
* Meanings: What do 'basic', 'simple', 'everyday' mean? Are they norm-related ('simple' for a 16-year-old – making tea under supervision)? What does 'complex' mean?

* Impossible leaps: how do you choose, say, the correct grade for Listening/Talking when the lowest grade is conceivably at the level of a 4-year-old and the highest two ('. . . effective . . . at interview' (2) and 'adept at . . . public speaking' (1) are challenging to experienced statesmen and television personalities? Similar problems exist in many categories.
* Untestable/unknowable characteristics: e.g.:

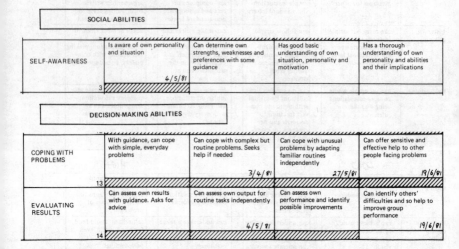

SOCIAL ABILITIES				
SELF-AWARENESS 3	Is aware of own personality and situation 4/5/81	Can determine own strengths, weaknesses and preferences with some guidance	Has good basic understanding of own situation, personality and motivation	Has a thorough understanding of own personality and abilities and their implications

DECISION-MAKING ABILITIES				
COPING WITH PROBLEMS 13	With guidance, can cope with simple, everyday problems	Can cope with complex but routine problems. Seeks help if needed 3/4/81	Can cope with unusual problems by adapting familiar routines independently 27/5/81	Can offer sensitive and effective help to other people facing problems 19/6/81
EVALUATING RESULTS 14	Can assess own results with guidance. Asks for advice	Can assess own output for routine tasks independently	Can assess own performance and identify possible improvements 4/5/81	Can identify others' difficulties and so help to improve group performance 19/6/81

Source: *Profiles*, op. cit.

Figure 9.6

Profiling 'Affective' Outcomes

An alternative approach to the assessment of affective outcomes – of a pupil's attitudes, interests, appreciations, values, emotions, social abilities, personality and so on – is to use a profile such as that in Figure 9.7 which incorporates comments from teachers. This is part of a recording scheme developed by CRAC, the highly respected Careers Research and Advisory Council.

Many teachers would prefer only to be involved in assessing observable behaviours, rather than making subjective judgements about personal qualities. It is much easier, for example, to comment objectively on the regularity of homework, on the observation of safe procedures in the lab.

Personal Assessment

School		Name		Forms group	55	Date of birth	20/3/57

Attitudes

Assertion	Very strong personality		As captain of the V year house football team he has managed the side well – although occasionally he has needed staff support.
	Fairly self assertive		
	Dominant only when occasion demands	✓	
	Usually prefers to avoid limelight		
	Passive almost negative		
Dependability	Exceptionally reliable	✓	If given a task for the school, house or himself he can be relied upon to see it through.
	Usually dependable		
	Reasonably dependable		
	Some doubt about dependability		
	Unreliable		
Initiative	Quick to seize opportunities and develop them		Will often come forward with ideas – and put these into practice. Hence his captaincy of football team, having suggested extra practices after school.
	Fairly resourceful, can make own decisions	✓	
	Can take initiative but prefers guidance		
	Inclined to play safe		
	Lets opportunities slip by. Little initiative		
Resilience	Exceptionally resilient copes under stress		His mother was recently ill in hospital: with aid of his elder sister coped very well.
	Usually takes problems in stride	✓	
	Manages fairly well under pressure		
	Does not cope well under pressure		
	May go to pieces under pressure		

Relationships

Co-operation	Exceptionally co-operative	✓	Never creates relationship problems.
	Very helpful		
	Reasonably amenable		
	Occasionally unco-operative		
	Sometimes difficult can be source of friction		
Friendship	Capable of mature friendships		Member of a group which has remained together for over 1½ years.
	Quite popular, makes friends easily		
	Has an average circle of friends	✓	
	Has some difficulty establishing relationships		
	Very shy and nervous, avoids others		
Leadership	Distinct management ability		Potentially a very good house prefect.
	Good at handing others		
	Has some success at getting the best out of people	✓	
	Prefers to be one of the group than lead it		
	Has not shown any leadership qualities		
Oral communication	Exceptionally fluent		
	Usually clear and precise		
	Reasonably clear powers of expression		
	Has some difficulty in communicating		
	Unable to communicate effectively		

Other attributes

Health	Normal	✓	Other information Has been an active member of the car mechanics club for two years, recently joined chemistry club:
	Health factors cause abnormal absence		
	Has required special consideration		

Attendance	Good	✓		Good	✓
	Satisfactory		Punctuality	Satisfactory	
	Poor			Poor	

Date	12-1-72	Signature	

Personal Assessment: ©CRAC 1971 Registration no: .... Expiry date: ....

Source: Personal Assessment. CRAC. 1971

Figure 9.7

or workshop, on the student's ability to plan her work or use reference materials, than it is to assess 'interest', 'effort' or 'co-operation'.

It may however be ncessary to have records, since employers and higher education are clearly interested in the affective domain: success in employment and learning depends crucially on commitment, interest, initiative, co-operation, stability and so on. Figure 9.8 is part of a form sent by ICI to the Head Teacher when a pupil applies for an engineering scholarship. Profiles are widely used in industrial training, not only to ensure that skills and course content is mastered, but to assess trainees for promotion.

CONFIDENTIAL REPORT FROM SCHOOL OR COLLEGE

ON_____

who has applied for a place on our studentship scheme, which provides for young people to take courses at university or polytechnic leading to the awarded of an honours degree in engineering (mechanical, chemical, electrical, electronic or civil) chemistry, physics or metallurgy. After training, an appointment as a professional engineer or scientist is envisaged, with prospects of promotion to middle and higher management positions.

1. Estimate of likely performance at GCE 'A' level or Scottish Certificate of Education (Higher level) or other examination e.g. Ordinary National Diploma

   a. Should achieve a good pass (i.e. 60%+) in

   b. Should pass in

   c. Doubtful pass in

2. Do you think this candidate is capable of obtaining a good honours degree?

3. Do you think this candidate could develop into a successful technical manager?

4. Assessment of candidate based on observation during school/college activities

The statements shown represent the extremes in each case. Please tick the appropriate column for each aspect.	1	2	3	4	5	6	
Has made fullest use of time at school							Has made only the minimum necessary effort
Has a very sensible attitude to authority							Inclined to be a troublemaker
Always gets on well with people							Solitary and unco-operative
A natural leader							Unable to lead or direct others
Has the drive to carry through difficult tasks							Easily put off by set backs or opposition
Always clear and concise in expression							Inarticulate or verbose
Written work always well-presented							Written work untidy and slipshod
Outstanding appreciation of theory							Unable to make obvious deductions from data
Quick to get to the root of a problem							Often misses the point
Outstanding at laboratory work							Poor at laboratory work

5. Head Teacher's Personal Report

Date   Signature

Name (BLOCK LETTERS) and Official Title   H.5443

Source: ICI (Engineering scholarship scheme).

Figure 9.8

It is possible to involve pupils in making these assessments. This topic is further discussed in Chapter 10, on Reports. If a student is aware that he or she will need a testimonial, or a profile in an UCCA form, and is involved in developing this (say, throughout the last two years at school), the process can have important formative benefits.

The Formative Use of Pupil Self-assessment

A student self-assessment profile such as the Clydebank sheet, shown in Figure 9.9 offers a structured approach to self assessment. It may have a role to play in diagnostic self-assessment provided it is supported by guidance and action. On the back of this sheet appeared open-ended sentences for student feedback at the end of learning modules:

MY COMMENTS
By doing this work I learnt . . . .
. . . .
. . . .
When doing this work the difficulties I had were . . . .
. . . .
. . . .
I think I could improve if . . . .
. . . .
. . . .
The things I enjoyed about this work were . . . .
. . . .
. . . .
I think my standard of work is. . . . .
. . . .
Signed. . . . . . . .Date . . . . .Teacher's Initials. . . . .

Teachers must be prepared to face the fact that some feedback can be negative. One teacher was surprised to discover that he was often inaudible: a fact his colleagues confirmed.

An even more open-ended approach is to include in the profile prepared by the teacher space for an active response from pupils. In Comberton Village College, for example, pupils are encouraged to write to their teacher about their interests, their pleasures and frustrations, ambitions and doubts in the subjects:

Clydebank EEC Project

Record of Personal Achievement

My name is.. My teacher is ....

This is my assessment of my work in...(Subject)

in the month(s) of......................19............

> *SELF–ASSESSMENT: I am responsible to myself for my own progress*
>
> *If my skills improve, I am the person most likely to benefit.*
>
> *If I do not develop my abilities, I am the person most likely to suffer.*

I am confident in these skills............

I am fairly confident in these.........

I find these skills difficult.........

I find these very difficult.....

		☺☺☺
LISTENING	Hearing, listening	☐☐☐☐
	Understanding what I hear	☐☐☐☐
	Following spoken instructions	☐☐☐☐
	'Learning from what I hear	☐☐☐☐
SPEAKING	Speaking clearly and pleasantly	☐☐☐☐
	Making my meaning clear	☐☐☐☐
	Asking useful questions	☐☐☐☐
	Saying interesting things	☐☐☐☐
READING	Making sense of print (words and letters) . .	☐☐☐☐
	Understanding books and newspapers . . .	☐☐☐☐
	Using books to widen my understanding . . .	☐☐☐☐
	Enjoying books and reading	☐☐☐☐
WRITING	Writing with good handwriting	☐☐☐☐
	Writing with good spelling, punctuation	☐☐☐☐
	Writing easy-to-read reports, letters, etc.	☐☐☐☐
	Writing interestingly and enjoyably	☐☐☐☐
REMEMBERING	Remembering things I have learnt in school . .	☐☐☐☐
	Making sense of what I remember	☐☐☐☐
	'Putting two and two together' – relating what I remember to new information	☐☐☐☐
USE OF DIAGRAMS, MAPS, GRAPHS	Understanding simple maps, signs, diagrams	☐☐☐☐
	Understanding more difficult maps, diagrams, train timetables, graphs, plans, etc.	☐☐☐☐
	Using and making my own sketches, graphs, etc.	☐☐☐☐
USE OF NUMBERS	Doing simple sums (+ − × ÷ =)	☐☐☐☐
	Doing practical sums (£ % ½ kilo cm lb)	☐☐☐☐
	Solving problems	☐☐☐☐
PHYSICAL CO-ORDINATION	Doing jobs that need strength or stamina . .	☐☐☐☐
	Skills like lifting, climbing, running	☐☐☐☐
	Taking part in sport, swimming, etc.	☐☐☐☐
	Enjoying leisure activities, dancing, etc.	☐☐☐☐
WORKING WITH	Skills like painting, cooking, woodwork	☐☐☐☐
	Using hand tools	☐☐☐☐
	Using power tools and equipment	☐☐☐☐
	Hobbies (e.g. art, playing a musical instrument)	☐☐☐☐

Source: Clydebank Project, Department of Education, Dunbarton Division Strathclyde.

Figure 9.9

> To Mr Blanchard   Date. . . . .
> I don't like it when we all have to read the same book together. I can't
> keep up sometimes and sometimes I want to carry on when we have to
> stop. I want to do more writing to make it neater. I like discussing
> problems but sometimes people just mess about.
>
> Tim Barrow   2S

A pupil can also make, in this school, a final statement about his or her
experience of the subject over the whole period of secondary schooling.
This is addressed to prospective employers or teachers, and forms part of
the student's profile, a complex document:

> To whom it may concern: A statement about my English work
> Although I have quite enjoyed reading novels, plays and poems in
> English, I really like to read factual books. My hobbies are collecting
> bottles, mending things and going for walks. I will always read a book
> about any of those things if I find one. I usually read the newspaper or
> part of it.
>
> I liked doing projects on my hobbies, especially on horses when I
> was horse mad. I never really got interested in writing stories. But I did
> like it when we wrote sort of poems about ourselves and other people.
>
> I want to work in a shop or an office and I think I can manage
> instructions in writing, writing letters and keeping records. My teachers
> and my mother say I am a tidy-minded person. My exam results won't
> be very special, but I have been trying to work for a CSE grade three.
>
> My folder shows all of my writing from the last two years. I choose
> the script and essay on the different ways different people talk and
> behave in shops as my best work. I wrote about managers, senior,
> junior and part-time assistants and of course most important of all –
> the customers. And I made a tape of the script.
>
> R. Darlow   Date . . . .

Source: John Blanchard: 'English at Comberton Village College', in Tyrrell
Burgess and Elizabeth Adams, *Outcomes of Education* (London:
Macmillan Education, 1980).

In other institutions the profile includes trainee-centred reviewing. Here
are the first dozen or so objectives from the fifty-odd offered to young
trainees:

TRAINEE SELF-REVIEW: GOALS (OBJECTIVES)

Which of the following would you say are reasons why you came to TFL or are goals (objectives) which you would like to achieve while on the scheme.

Personal

To get to know myself better.
To like myself more.
To become more confident.
To become more self-disciplined.
To know more about what I want to do with my life.
      (12 more objectives)

Leisure

To know the range of spare-time open to me.
To know where these can be done, how much they would cost me.
To know how to arrange holidays.
      (4 more objectives)

Work

To get to know the sort of job I would like.
To know the sort of job that would suit me.
To want to get a job more.
To want to go to work more.
To enjoy work more.
      (8 more objectives)

Other issues

To know more about:
Law and the police.
Rights and responsibilities.
Race relations.
Politics and government.
      (5 more objectives)

Source: B. Pearce *et al., Trainee Centred Reviewing: Helping Trainees to Help Themselves*, MSC Research and Development Series No 2, Nov 1981.

In this kind of student-centred assessment the individual is encouraged to identify his or her own learning goals, through discussion with his tutor, and then define the criteria for attainment. The approach works well in individualised learning, such as most sixth-form work, community service projects or work experience, and individual and group projects from computer programming to remedial learning.

Profile Assessment in Personal, Curricular and Vocational Guidance

If a young person fails to identify his or her own learning goals, he or she is unlikely to move very purposefully forward. Probably the majority of pupils have no clear learning objectives. Profiles may clarify these.

In school there is often a rather poor fit between the school's learning goals and young persons' goals. Only a minority of pupils work single-mindedly for the official goals: academic success at 'O' and 'A' levels. For many pupils the traditional school assessment system, with its norm-related ranking, is incongruous. Its feedback for at least half the pupils (the below-average) is largely negative. They protect themselves from the stigma of being 'thick' by the myth that they might have got better marks if they had worked. But they contravene the pupil code if they do work. Work threatens their mates, for in a norm-referenced system your success is won by improving your relative position at the expense of your mates. Brilliance is forgiveable, but work is not. A pupil who works is a 'swot', a 'snob', a 'teacher's pet', and socially unacceptable. This code results in considerable under-achievement, particularly in the middle school, even among above-average pupils.

Profiled assessment may be much less threatening to the pupil code, since it emphasises competencies, attainments, skills and aptitudes. A grade like D or E in a traditional test is a macho symbol for a 14-year-old. A detailed profile identifying attainable goals, monitoring progress in achieving these and suggesting where and how improvement is necessary and possible, is not so easily shrugged off. The pupil is competing not with his or her mates but with himself for mastery. The success of one pupil increases the likelihood of success for others.

Learning Goals

Profiling can also offer learning goals that seem to pupils far more relevant to their personal development than much academic activity which they see (and not without reason) as second-hand processing of outdated information, through memorisation, repetition and copying. Figure 9.10 shows lifelong learning goals which most teenagers and most adults would recognise as of prime importance to themselves.

Such lifelong learning goals are clearly not examinable through traditional school assessment systems. If they are educational (as well as learning) goals, they can however be assessed diagnostically by the young person, using, perhaps, a format similar to that of the Clydebank self-

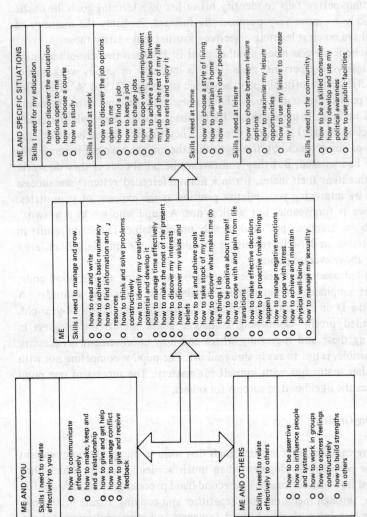

ME AND YOU

Skills I need to relate effectively to you

○ how to communicate effectively
○ how to make, keep and end a relationship
○ how to give and get help
○ how to manage conflict
○ how to give and receive feedback

ME

Skills I need to manage and grow

○ how to read and write
○ how to achieve basic numeracy
○ how to find information and resources
○ how to think and solve problems constructively
○ how to identify my creative potential and develop it
○ how to manage time effectively
○ how to make the most of the present
○ how to discover my interests
○ how to discover my values and beliefs
○ how to set and achieve goals
○ how to take stock of my life
○ how to discover what makes me do the things I do
○ how to be positive about myself
○ how to cope with and gain from life transitions
○ how to make effective decisions
○ how to be proactive (make things happen)
○ how to manage negative emotions
○ how to cope with stress
○ how to achieve and maintain physical well-being
○ how to manage my sexuality

ME AND OTHERS

Skills I need to relate effectively to others

○ how to be assertive
○ how to influence people and systems
○ how to work in groups
○ how to express feelings constructively
○ how to build strengths in others

ME AND SPECIFIC SITUATIONS

Skills I need for my education

○ how to discover the education options open to me
○ how to choose a course
○ how to study

Skills I need at work

○ how to discover the job options open to me
○ how to find a job
○ how to keep a job
○ how to change jobs
○ how to cope with unemployment
○ how to achieve a balance between my job and the rest of my life
○ how to retire and enjoy it

Skills I need at home

○ how to choose a style of living
○ how to maintain a home
○ how to live with other people

Skills I need at leisure

○ how to choose between leisure options
○ how to maximise my leisure opportunities
○ how to use my leisure to increase my income

Skills I need in the community

○ how to be a skilled consumer
○ how to develop and use my political awareness
○ how to use public facilities

© Counselling and Career Development Unit, University of Leeds.

Figure 9.10 Learning goals (life skills)

assessment sheet (Figure 9.9), where the student identifies areas where he or she feels confident, and areas where support and guidance are needed. The value of a profile of this kind is that, with guidance, it can become a basis for reflection, discussion and action. Sensitively used, such profiles can be extremely helpful to students. They can remain entirely private, or shared with a trusted adult.

Careers Education and Counselling

Profiles also offer a method of matching the student's strengths and weaknesses, abilities, interests and aptitudes, with those required in various jobs, or in the training and education for various vocations. This type of profiling is already widely used.

There are also by now a number of computer-based careers programs which do just this, such as CASCAID, DEVAT and JIIG-CAL, Computajob (CRAC). In the JIIG-CAL system, pupils fill out responses to questionnaires in careers lessons. These are sent to a central computer, and some weeks later a printout is returned giving a profile of the pupil's interests and aptitudes, and job-profiles which match well with these, at a level determined by the young person, who specifies how long she/he is prepared to train.

Profile Reports for School-leavers

The swing towards summative profiled reports for school-leavers comes with the realisation that a certification system designed for the academically gifted minority cannot provide an adequate educational goal for the talents and interests of the whole population as it passes through the secondary school.

No school considering introducing profiles for school-leavers can afford to ignore the Schools Council publications on this topic: *Recording achievement at 16+* and *Profile Reports for School-leavers*. Among other publications, in particular, I would recommend *Pupils in Profile*, the SCRE report which started the ball rolling; and the Further Education Unit's *Profiles*. Full details of these appear in the Bibliography. These books provide many and various models, which can be adapted to differing circumstances.

Profiles would appear to offer a more relevant, individual and comprehensive statement of a school-leaver's achievements than either a certificate merely showing GCE results, or the absence of any statements. In some areas, notably Oxfordshire, work is going on to develop leavers' certificates. The Oxford Certificate of Educational Achievement (OCEA) is, at the time of writing, still in a developmental stage. It will include first a record of success in external examinations – everything from GCE and CSE to BEC/TEC and CGLI. Next it will include the results of graded assessments (at first under the headings of English, Mathematics, Science and Modern Languages). It may also include graded non-scholastic achievements, such as graded tests in music, shorthand, life-saving, or, for that matter, Scout badges and the Duke of Edinburgh awards. Lastly, the certificate will include a personal profile of the pupil's achievements in and out of school. The aim is, to use an Oxford buzz-phrase, to provide 'a celebration of success'.

Profiled reports of school-leavers often attempt a summative assessment in two areas: basic skills and work-related attitudes.

One approach is to leave the students to check out their basic skills, as in the Evesham High School checklists, two of which appear in Figure 9.11. A member of staff validates this. To this might be added a testimonial such as the William Penn testimonial (a document jointly developed by the student and his/her tutor) which is discussed in Chapter 10 on Reports.

Alternatively, you can go for the summative profile used by SCRE or an adaptation of the CGLI Vocational Preparation grid (Figure 9.12) (pp. 168–9).

Profiles for External Examinations

Some of my examples have already been drawn from external examinations, since the search for a nationally valid means of certification based on student profiles is already having a 'backwash' effect on the school curriculum and assessment strategies.

I have already expressed reservations about grid profiles (see p. 155). A careful study of the CGLI Vocational Preparation grid used to profile attainments in Basic Abilities (Figure 9.12) will reveal a considerable number of problem areas. Nevertheless, it needs to be asked, does not this type of continuous assessment offer many of our pupils a more detailed, more relevant and more broadly based assessment of the learning outcomes of their eleven years' compulsory schooling than a traditional academic examination in which they at best will get a single-grade mark (A, B, C, etc.)?

Should schools enter pupils for this type of examination? This depends on two factors. Does the course and assessment fit in with the school's learning objectives? And will the profile serve school-leavers well – has it

Language skills

	Staff	Stamp
1. Has legible handwriting		
2. Can write simple sentences		
3. Can read and understand a popular newspaper		
4. Can use simple punctuation correctly		
5. Avoids elementary spelling mistakes		
6. Can write a personal letter		
7. Can give and take a telephone message		
8. Can accurately complete a passport application		
9. Regularly borrows from school or public library		
10. Can write a business letter		
11. Can make an accurate written report		
12. Can make a clear spoken report		
13. Can summarise accurately a notice or report		
14. Can understand simple instructions in a foreign language		
15. Can give simple instructions in a foreign language		

Maths skills

	Staff	Stamp
1. Has a good understanding of the rules of number		
2. Has a good accuracy in handling numbers		
3. Can apply the four rules to money with accuracy		
4. Capable of performing every-day calculations in money with accuracy		
5. Understands money transactions such as wages and income tax		
6. Able to handle decimals met in every-day life		
7. Able to handle fractions met in every-day life		
8. Understands simple percentages		
9. Understands profit and loss		
10. Understands metric system of measure		
11. Understands English measures of length, weight and capacity		
12. Can measure accurately		
13. Is able to use a calculator		
14. Has an understanding of V.A.T.		
15. Can read and understand time tables, wage tables and ready reckoner		

Figure 9.11 Evesham High School leavers' profile (part only)

City and Guilds of London Institute
365 VOCATIONAL PREPARATION (GENERAL)

Attainments in basic abilities

		4 (Basic Level)	3	2	1 (High Level)
SOCIAL ABILITIES	WORKING WITH COLLEAGUES	Can co-operate with others when led	Can work with other members of group to achieve common aims 10/3/81	Understands own position and results of own actions within a group 15/6/81	Is an active, decisive member of group. Helps and encourages others
	WORKING WITH THOSE IN AUTHORITY	Can follow verbal instructions for simple tasks and can perform them under supervision 17/3/81	Can follow a series of verbal instructions and carry them out independently	Can carry out a series of tasks effectively, given minimum instructions 15/6/81	Inspires confidence in those in authority and communicates well with them
	SELF-AWARENESS	Is aware of own personality and situation 4/5/81	Can determine own strengths, weaknesses and preferences with some guidance	Has good basic understanding of own situation, personality and motivation	Has a thorough understanding of own personality and abilities and their implications
COMMUNICATION	TALKING AND LISTENING	Can hold conversations with workmates, face-to-face or by phone. Can take messages 12/1/81	Can follow and give simple descriptions and explanations	Can communicate effectively with a range of people in a variety of situations 17/6/81	Can present a logical and effective argument. Can analyse other's arguments
	READING AND WRITING	Can understand and write simple notices, labels and short notes	Can follow and give straightforward written instructions and explanations	Can use instruction manuals and can write reports describing work done 4/5/81	Can select and criticise written data and use it to produce own written work
	VISUAL UNDERSTANDING	Can interpret simple signs and indicators 4/5/81	Can, after guidance, make use of basic graphs, charts, tables, drawings, etc.	Can interpret and use basic graphs, charts, tables and drawings unaided	Can construct graphs, etc., and extract information to support arguments

PRACTICAL & NUMERICAL ABILITIES				
7 USING EQUIPMENT	After demonstration, can use equipment safely to perform simple tasks	With guidance, can use equipment safely to perform multi-step tasks 18/5/81	Can select and use suitable equipment and materials for the job, without help	Can set up and maintain equipment. Can identify/remedy common faults
8 DEXTERITY AND CO-ORDINATION	Can use everyday implements, can lift, carry and set down objects as directed	Can reliably perform basic manipulative tasks 18/6/81	Can perform complex tasks requiring accuracy and dexterity	Can perform tasks requiring a high degree of manipulative control
9 MEASURING	Can read graduated linear scales and dials	Can measure out specified quantities of material by length, weight, etc. 5/3/81	Can set up and use simple precision instruments 18/4/81	Can set up and use complex precision instruments 15/6/81
10 CALCULATING	Can identify size, shape, order etc. Can add and subtract whole numbers	Can use $+/-/\times/\div$ to solve single-step, whole number problems. Can estimate 8/3/81	Can use $+/-/\times/\div$ to solve two-step problems. Can add and subtract decimals	Can use $+/-/\times/\div$ to solve multi-step problems. Can multiply and divide decimals 15/6/81
DECISION-MAKING ABILITIES				
11 PLANNING	After demonstration, can identify the sequence of steps in a routine task 3/2/81	Can choose from given alternatives the best way of tackling a task	Can modify/extend given plans/routines to meet changed circumstances 17/3/81	Can create new plans/routines from scratch, using all sources of help 16/6/81
12 INFORMATION SEEKING	Can find information with guidance from supervisor	Can use standard sources of information 2/3/81	Can assemble information from several sources 18/4/81	Shows initiative in seeking and gathering information from a wide variety of sources 3/6/81
13 COPING WITH PROBLEMS	With guidance, can cope with simple, everyday problems	Can cope with complex but routine problems. Seeks help if needed 3/4/81	Can cope with unusual problems by adapting familiar routines independently 27/5/81	Can offer sensitive and effective help to other people facing problems 19/6/81
14 EVALUATING RESULTS	Can assess own results with guidance. Asks for advice	Can assess own output for routine tasks independently 4/5/81	Can assess own performance and identify possible improvements	Can identify others' difficulties and so help to improve group performance 19/6/81

Source: Profiles, Further Education Curriculum Review and Development Unit

Figure 9.12

respectability and credibility in the job market? Many would argue that profiles do not have the universal currency of norm-related grades – the trademarks of GCE and CSE.

In times of high unemployment, however, selection on the basis of norm-related examination grades is not easy. Many employers like profiles. With hundreds of applicants for, say, a clerical, manual or technician job, the employer must pick not the 'best' academically (the 57 arts graduates, presumably), but the most suitable. Profiles should ideally, employers argue, state what the young person knows and can do, against a defined standard, and how he compares with his peer group.

Has Profiling a Future?

Whether profiling is extensively adopted throughout the education system is far from certain. It is likely to be strongly resisted by traditionalists, who see the familiar examination system, with its academic priorities, threatened by the movement. Examinations have become associated with the maintenance of curricular and pedagogic standards. They are, it is argued, a convenient, credible, impersonal yardstick of proven worth.

Moreover, all change is disorientating. Profiling requires major reorientation. In many cases it requires a reconsideration of aims and objectives, a possible switch from a norm-related frame of reference to criterion-referencing, and far greater priority being given to educational goals for all children, not just the elite destined for higher education.

Quite apart from resistance to change there are real problems in profiling:

* Profiling is time-consuming. It involves, in some forms, tedious administrative and clerical procedures, although intelligent use of computers would reduce this.
* Profiling demands attention to the less able. The assessment of high flyers (setting and marking mock 'O' and 'A' level examinations, and homework) has been seen as status-giving and 'worth while'; assessment of the less able is widely regarded as tedious and unrewarding.
* Profiling is low-status. Because of the pressing assessment needs of the less able, profiling has concentrated on below-average pupils. This has tended to devalue profiles as an assessment strategy for all pupils.
* Profiling demands subjective assessments. Examinations and tests are allegedly objective, and profiles feared as subjective, value-laden, and

unreliable. (Examinations, however, are neither a valid nor a reliable way of assessing many worth-while learning outcomes.)

* Profiling is in a state of flux. There are so many shapes and sizes, so many approaches and philosophies, that it lacks national validity. This is still true, at the time of writing.
* Profiling is unpopular with industry. This is not true. Industy is by and large enthusiastic, and uses profiling extensively in training. Profiles are more reliable and valid as assessments of most school-leavers entering employment.

Why then, if there are so many problems, are many schools involved in developing profiles?

Part of the answer seems to be that the consumers of education – the public, employers, even parents and young people – are demanding greater accountability from the system. Marks or grades are inscrutable. Examinations, such as 'O' levels, are under attack as 'exclusive, trivial, uninformative, expensive, misused and in many ways, anti-educational' (to quote from Tyrrel Burgess and Elizabeth Adams's *Outcomes of Education*, 1980). Profiling, because it relates to curricular objectives and is concerned with learning outcomes, is more open and responsible, it is argued.

The thrust towards profiling comes at least as much from the teaching profession, despite the problems it brings with it. The examples I have quoted show the variety of purposive experiments being made in this field. Teachers using profiles are often enthusiastic.

A powerful incentive for the development of profiles is that the computer may prove a considerable assistance. Computers are particularly good at criterion-referenced assessment (comparing the pupil's performance against the required standard).

Computer-assisted profiling would go a long way to resolving the greatest single objection to profiling: the demands on teacher time. It will not solve the time-consuming problems of sorting out your objectives and defining the criteria for success. These, however, present teachers with challenges and opportunities which many would welcome. But computers can largely eliminate tedious clerical chores – marking up grids, collating profiles and so on.

The use of computers in assessment raises fears, however, about secret computerised files.This fear is not without foundation. If pupil profiles are stored on computers, arguably there should be open access to the profile by the pupil and his parents, and the opportunity to modify the profile if it is factually incorrect.

Conclusion

Perhaps it is significant that we ourselves, when we are being assessed, would be ill-satisfied with a conflated mark or grade. How would we react to 'Failed, 85 per cent' as the only feedback from a driving test ('where did I go wrong?'), or 'Health, 67 per cent after a medical examination ('What's the matter with me?'). If, as in so many professions, there were regular assessments of our professional performance, could we accept a bald conflated mark that sets us above the unfortunate Mr X in the Physics Department, but way below Miss Y in PE? Or would we demand a detailed, systematic, relevant, informative, individual profile of our skills, knowledge and understandings? If we would demand this for ourselves, do our pupils deserve less?

10

Reports to Parents

The communication of assessment, through school reports to parents and other related reporting, is a strangely neglected area of assessment, and indeed of school life in general. The first major study of this crucial area, *School Reports to Parents* by Brian Goacher and Margaret Reid (NFER-Nelson), was published as recently as 1983. Almost without exception, books on assessment have been totally silent on the topic. This seems to suggest that the communication of assessment is widely regarded as an unimportant ritual: school reports are seen as time-consuming (unfortunately) for staff, but only weakly connected with the real business of assessment.

I shall argue that in fact the school report is a pivotal point in the recording, communication and use of assessment. Reports epitomise the educational priorities of the school. If the school has no clear priorities in assessment, reports will reflect the lack of a school policy. They are the outward and (to parents) visible sign of an in-school and largely invisible process; the process of assessment. We devalue all in-school assessment if we act as if the public examination certificate is the only valid communication on assessment. Throughout the child's schools career report after report offers a point of engagement between the three most important participants in education – the child, the school and the home. Each report thus offers a unique opportunity to translate the whole process of assessment into an individualised plan for each child, with the backing of informed parents, to achieve educational and personal objectives.

Schools, whether they have a policy on assessment and reporting or not, have to put a great deal of effort into the organisation of reports. The co-ordination of the whole reporting process calls for administrative expertise. The procedure varies from school to school, depending on resources, staffing and technology. One school's solution would be unlikely to work in another. I do not propose therefore to discuss the administrative procedures. The NFER research project I have already mentioned (*School Reports to Parents*, 1983) deals with the practice in schools at the time of the research project. It gives the fine detail that is impossible in a single chapter. Moreover, recommendations on the administrative aspects of reporting procedure would date very rapidly, as computer technology transforms the recording, collation and communication of information that lies at the heart of assessment.

The key question is, however, not one of organisation (who is responsible for which aspects? how is the procedure to be administered?) nor of technology. It is not even one of timing (autumn? spring? summer?) or of format (single-page? booklet of slips? profile?). It is one of function. Who is the report for? What is it intended to achieve? From this flows any consideration of how reports are, or should be, integrated with curricular objectives and assessment criteria on the one hand, and home-school communication on the other.

The classroom teacher is often too busy to ask the crucial questions about function. School traditions and assumptions are not questioned. And what, after all, is the point in asking questions about function if you are not in a position to change the system, including format and timing? There is, I believe, quite a lot of room for manoeuvre within present reporting systems. For example, the space on a report slip can be used with great effect. One of the major concerns of this chapter is how individual teachers, individual departments and teachers with pastoral responsibilities, can initiate changes and improve the quality of their own reports, within the present set up, through a better understanding of the function of reports.

A second major concern in this chapter is how function (a basic question of educational philosophy) needs to be considered before changes are made in administration, timing and format. Change is inevitable. It will be forced on schools by the introduction of new technology, by changes on a national scale in assessment and public examinations and by pressures for greater accountability to the public and, in particular, to parents. These pressures will cause schools to reshape their reporting procedures. Unless the question of function is carefully considered decisions will be made which owe more to fashion than to substance.

The questions raised in this chapter are thus relevant to individual teachers concerned with the quality of their current reporting, and to head teachers, school working parties, school governors and indeed parents, planning new reporting systems and approaches.

Let us begin by looking at two contrasting approaches to reporting, which I shall call the 'basic information model' and the 'involvement

Assessment: From Principles to Action

model' (following the classification of a number of recent studies of home–school communications).

Traditional School Reports: Basic Information

The traditional school report (the report familiar to parents from their own schooldays) follows what has been called the 'basic information model'. A typical report of the old school type centres on aspects such as high spirits, talkativeness and a certain lack of application. Typical comments in such a report might be:

'Cheery . . . ' 'Asks too many questions . . . ' 'Asks too many irrelevant questions . . . ' 'Rather flippant . . . ' 'Contentious but at least he has the power of speech. Does not work for long.'

The pupil's parents, it seems, must urge him to improve his position relative to the other pupils. He can achieve this alledgedly by paying more attention. In fact his success in improving his position depends on the relative performance of the other pupils who are, no doubt, likewise spurred on to compete. But what happens to the pupil when he does try?

'French: Finds French a struggle but tries.'
'Physics: Rather a disappointing mark considering the interest he shows.'

No guidance is offered here.

A more up-to-date computerised version is that in Figure 10.1. Notice that although the comments lack the quirky individuality of some of our fictional pupil's mentors, they are still based on the same premises: they are norm-related summative reports. Their function is to inform parents about how their daughter or son has done in relation to other children in the class.

In both cases the purpose is to convey to parents necessary information about their child's progress – necessary, that is, in the eyes of the school. This type of report usually includes an attendance total, and marks or, more commonly nowadays, grades for attainment and a grade for effort in each subject. These are followed, in most cases, with a brief conventional comment from subject teachers on progress, effort, attitude and behaviour. The brevity of the comments (necessitated by inadequate space) often tempts teachers to resort either to clichés ('Could try harder') or educa-

EDUCATION AUTHORITY
****

COMPREHENSIVE SCHOOL
****

HEADMASTER
****

REPORT FOR YEAR ENDING JULY 21ST 1978   NAME   FORM
***   ******   ******

Subject	Year Mark	Exam Mark	Posn in set	Comment	Teacher
ENGLISH	68	61	06/29 Set	A good examination result. Has tried very hard this year.	Mrs
WELSH	65	58	01/32 Set 03	A fairly good examination result. Has made encouraging progress this year.	Mrs
FRENCH	68	61	04/29 Set	A good examination result. Has worked adequately through the year.	Mrs
HISTORY	40	76	06/31 Set 01	A very good examination result. Always works well. Shows much promise.	Mrs
GEOGRAPHY	51	59	02/29 Set	A good examination result. Needs constant perseverance in class and homework.	Mrs
REL. INSTRUCTION	43	52	08/29 Set	A rather poor examination result. Needs constant perseverance in class and homework.	Mrs
PHYSICS	84	56	10/29 Set	A good examination result. Has worked well through the year.	Mr
CHEMISTRY	55	49	06/29 Set 03	A fair examination result. Has shown much promise this year.	Mr
BIOLOGY	53	59	08/29 Set	A good examination result. Has worked adequately through the year.	Mrs
MATHEMATICS	67	58	17/34 Set 01	A fair examination result. Has progressed satisfactorily this year.	Mr
ART	50	58	06/29 Set	A good examination result. Has made encouraging progress this year.	Mr
MUSIC	60	91	01/29 Set 03	An excellent examination result. Always works well. Shows much promise.	Miss
BOYS' PRACTICAL	62	74	01/16 Set	An excellent examination result. Always works well. Shows much promise.	Mr
P.E.	52		/ Set	Fair. Has shown a keen interest this year.	Mr

REMARKS: CONDUCT:
*********   ********

ATTENDANCE: POSSIBLE 397 ACTUAL
               Form Teacher: Mrs   Head of School: Mrs
               Schools' Computer Centre
****

Figure 10.1

tional shorthand impenetrable to parents. The single sheet also encourages teachers to echo one another's comments (as in Nicholas's report, which is a real example); sometimes it is tempting to indulge in exhibitions of schoolmaster wit intended more for your colleagues delight than parents' information:

'Her original spelling is a constant challenge to the interpretive ingenuities of her mentors.'

'His discretion in placing the most pungent of his graffiti on the least obvious part of the desk is to be admired. His illustrations would be a credit to any biology book.'

Most 'basic information' reports conclude with a slightly longer general comment from the form or house tutor, which can be anodyne or caustic, according to taste.

When a school replaces the older single-sheet report with a booklet of slips, but leaves unchanged the traditional functions of the 'basic information model' report, teachers' comments, though longer, often have little meaning and are unconstructive:

'Grade for term: C. Exam mark: 47 per cent.'
'Brian's progress in this subject has been fairly satisfactory during the year. He still experiences difficulty in one or two areas and needs to try harder. He is easily distracted, but if he can put in more effort he may achieve an adequate result in his examinations this summer.'

A fellow teacher reading this readily senses the report writer's exasperation. But what message does the parent get? There is no attempt to identify the 'areas of weakness'. They could be any aspect of the boy's work – skills such as spelling, taking notes, handling statistics, practical work, map work, essays, exam. technique; knowledge of particular topics; or possibly behaviour in class. The generalised exhortation to 'try harder' is likely to be ineffective. How? Is homework the problem? classwork? revision? And how is the parent to help? Mother and father can lean heavily on Brian, urge him to try harder. But what else?

The reason for the poor quality of the 'basic information' comments may be that the traditional school report, although nominally addressed to parents, is very much a school document: its concerns, priorities and terms of reference are those of the school as an institution, rather than those of parents concerned about their own child. Its perspective is that of the school (children are 'pupils', knowledge is compartmentalised into 'subject'). It is often encoded in school language. For example, most teachers would use 'easily distracted' as code for 'a nuisance in class'; most parents would read it as 'misled by other children'. Indeed, many teachers may be so aware of the initial readers of the report (the head of department, the house tutor and probably the head teacher) that the parental audience is rather overlooked.

Teachers in schools issuing traditional reports are somewhat sceptical about the effectiveness of reporting. This is not entirely surprising. The formal report was evolved in an age when an authoritarian hierarchy such as the grammar school could demand, and often received, the support of another authority figure, the parent. Conditions have changed. The formal tone of the report, which once commanded respect, now only serves to distance many parents.

Second, summative reports, which of necessity come at the end of a year (or term), are timed to make the minimum impact on present performance. Good resolutions about future work wither over the summer.

Third, the parent brings to the reading of his or her child's report the understandings he or she gained as a school child fifteen to thirty years ago. Yet the educational changes that have occurred since parents left school are massive, and disorientating. Nor is the pace of change likely to slow down in the remainder of this century. Teachers, who live with these changes, learn to adjust and, in due course, forget that not everyone knows about foundation courses, mixed ability teaching or criterion-referenced assessment. The traditional school report assumes that parents have no 'need to know' about these changes, need little guidance in adjusting to them, have no expertise to contribute and indeed have only a marginal role in the education of their child.

Involvement and the 'Need to Know'

The 'basic information' report gives little guidance to parents on many questions of great importance to them and their children. It is inscrutable because the marks, grades and eliptical comments have little content and convey few meaningful messages.

Does this matter to parents? Most ordinary parents have as a bench-mark for their children's reports, their memories of their own school days, so their expectation is a traditional report. Apparently as recently as the late 1970s a majority of parents in the NFER study to which I have already referred were fairly satisfied with the amount information in reports about their child's progress (81 per cent agreed that the amount of information was 'about right', although one in five still thought that the information was 'inadequate'). Just over 70 per cent of parents felt that there was adequate information on their child's ability, and on their child as a person (although three out of ten parents felt the information on these two aspects was inadequate). However, 56 per cent felt that information on what their child learnt was inadequate, 61 per cent felt they needed more information on the teaching group, 53 per cent wanted more information on 'O' level/CSE chances, and no less than 79 per cent were dissatisfied with the amount of information reports gave on their child's career chances or FE chances. Not a single parent, out of the 1375 consulted, felt that they were given 'excessive information' in any of these categories.

Clearly, parents yearn for more information. Each report is a uniquely important document to parents because it is the only written communication from the school which concentrates solely and fully on their own child, offering a composite picture, from many hands, of how their child performs. Many parents would like some understanding of the following questions:

* What has my son or daughter learned this year (or this term)?
* What are you actually assessing?
* How do you assess my child's progress?
* What are your standards?
* How can my son or daughter improve his/her work?
* What can you tell me about the potential of my son or daughter?
* What do my son's (or daughter's) grades mean in terms of educational and vocational goals?
* Is my child reasonably happy and fulfilled at school?
* How can we, as parents, help our child to succeed?

These are questions which parents have a right to ask, and schools a duty to consider during the reporting process. They also probe the school's own assessment priorities.

To some extent an individual teacher, working within the limitations of the report slip and the follow-up interviews at parents' evenings, can respond. It is a great deal easier if the school's policy is to try to shape its reporting procedures to answer the parents.

In responding it is not necessary to use esoteric jargon, which is confusing to almost all parents (and not a few teachers). Nor is it essential to be immensely wordy, which is unlikely to be successful in communicating with parents from different ethnic backgrounds. But it is necessary to see reports as the core of an extended home–school dialogue. They should be designed to do a particular job in this wider context, closely linked with consultative meetings involving parents as partners.

But What About the Time Factor?

An immediate objection to 'involvement reporting', which must spring into the mind of every practising teacher, is the one of time. Reports are always written under great pressure (although schools which carefully spread the process can somewhat ease the burden). Is it fair to ask teachers to undertake more than the 'basic information' type of reporting?

This, surely, is a question of priorities.

We usually see our first priority as teachers as teaching – covering the syllabus. We can be so pre-occupied with this that we persist in teaching even at the expense of good learning. We might usefully consider whether good learning (which implies formative assessment) may not be more important at times than teaching. We may have to sacrifice teaching time to learning time. Reports are important to learning, and should at times take precedence over teaching.

Second, a very considerable amount of time is spent by conscientious teachers in marking – marking classwork, marking homework, marking examinations. Some sense of proportion is necessary. Because marking is done week in, week out, it is in a way a normal part of a teacher's workload. Not so reporting. It is the extra burden which is resented, even though, over a year, far more time is devoted to marking. Yet assessment is a rather pointless activity if the mark book, rather than the report, is the end-product. We may need at times to sacrifice marking to reporting.

Here clear guidance is probably needed from the headteacher and heads of departments on the priorities for teaching, assessing and reporting. Traditional reports were time-consuming enough. If now, to improve learning, a school is moving towards newer and more comprehensive forms of reporting, it needs to recognise that the burden of serious reporting is real. Teachers should be offered in-service training, if they desire it, and extra time for writing reports, at the expense, if necessary, of teaching and routine marking.

Involvement Models of Reports

If we decide to go ahead with reporting which will involve pupils and their parents we need to be aware that 'involvement reports' may be geared either to formative or developmental assessment. The choice depends on the stage of the child's schooling.

Formative Assessment in School Reports

Formative assessment (in the sense in which it has been used throughout this book) is concerned with feedback during the course of the learning experience, with assessment as a support for, and stimulus to, good learning. Compare, for example, these two comments on performance in art quoted by Michael Marland:

'Angela works well.'

'Vicky's textures are good, but her proportions need care.'

Source: Michael Marland, *Pastoral Care* (London: Heinemann, 1974).

The first comment is typical of a 'basic information' report; the second is a 'quality' comment, giving good feedback.

Teachers, aware that determination and motivation is extremely relevant to success in achieving goals, frequently use reports to exhort pupils, in a very generalised way, to greater effort. This usually has a rather short-lived effect.

You need to be sensitive about the effect of feedback. Contrast the quality of the advice in two reports on the same child in Figure 10.2: one shows a lack of empathy that made it completely counter-productive: the child, shown in the mirror of the report as 'sullen', became yet more withdrawn and unco-operative. She still had problems some years later but note how her economics teacher encourages her to enter into class discussions: the more constructive self-image was helpful to this unconfident youngster.

Individual teachers can, and do, use 'quality' comments to improve their students' learning, but they are restricted by the format (there is more space on a slip than a single-page report sheet) and constrained by factors they cannot control, such as timing.

This is where schools rather than individual teachers must take the initiative.

Formative reports, for example, need to be timed so that they offer the maximum opportunities for parents to back their children in the

Name Mary TAYLOR............... Subject ECONOMICS...

Date February 1983................ Level A...........

Examination Result 63%........

Estimated 'A' Level equivalent Grade B/A

Essays 56% Multiple Choice 72% Statistical 65%

.... came top in the examination in her group.
She performed very well under pressure of time in the
statistical interpretation questions and in the multiple choice paper,
but her essays contained some remarkable errors which
suggest that she simply needs to know her material more thoroughly.

I am glad that she is now readier to enter class discussion. Her
homework essays continue to be of minimal length; she could
afford to allow herself some elaboration of points

Subject french

Name Samantha Jones Class 4B   Teaching group 4C

It is obvious from her written work that she has ability.
She has been too inhibited to make any contribution to
the oral work in the class. It is a painfull process
extracting an answer in French or English and one
is continually met with a sullen expression, when
seeking a response from her

Signature Michael Graham

Figure 10.2 Productive and counter-productive comments on the same
child

endeavour to improve performance, build upon strengths and remedy weaknesses. For this reason such reports will usually be mid-course reports.

Schools which see reports as giving feedback to parents and pupils may also offer parents an explanation of the context of the report. The report from St Columba's High School (Figure 10.3) is an example. (Unfortunately the 'further comment' has been deleted in this interesting example.) Notice how this department has worked out the curricular objectives, and how the profiled report relates to these. Learning outcomes are explained in a way that helps both parents and child to understand what the course is about, and what are the criteria for the assessment. This is the kind of report which can evolve by a departmental working party within a school, given backing from the head teacher.

In addition, the format influences the outcomes of reporting. Reports are most likely to achieve something if they can offer specific, detailed, and constructive guidance. A section headed 'Action' on each report slip is a format that focuses the mind of teacher, student and the parental back-up team.

Developmental Reports

At certain times in pupils' school careers schools should design reports as developmental, rather than formative: reporting within the context of important curricular, vocational or personal developments for the student.

Most schools, for example, time reports for the third year so that these initiate discussions on course options for the last two years of compulsory schooling. They may seek to identify aptitudes, characteristics and interests that will contribute to a pupil's success in one subject or another. They may well attempt some indication of the potential of the student. Here are guidelines printed by one school on reports preceding selecting options for fourth year:

> Your choice of options for your fourth and fifth year depends on the interest you have in the subject and how well you hope to do. So we have given you a grade based on the level we think you could achieve if you work for the next two years to the best of your ability.

GRADE ON REPORT	PREDICTED EXAM GRADE
1	'O' level: A/B Possible A level
2	'O' level: B/C
3	'O' level: C/D CSE 1
4	CSE 2/3
6	Foundation level course

ASSESSMENT RECORD OF $\boxed{\text{ANGELA}}$ OF CLASS $\boxed{2A}$ IN MODERN STUDIES

DATE: $\boxed{\text{DECEMBER, 1982}}$

Dear Parent,

This is the first of two reports you will receive about how your child is coping with Modern Studies. You will receive the second report in MARCH, 1983.

In second year, the pupils have been studying the concept of AUTHORITY. Examples have been taken from LOCAL GOVERNMENT, THE GOVERNMENT OF GREAT BRITAIN, and THE E.E.C. This has involved the following activities: listening to lessons and answering oral questions; reading and understanding Worksheets and giving written answers to set questions; acting in small plays and presenting material graphically (drawing, making simple maps and diagrams).

Most of the work has involved the completion of the worksheets. These are divided into three categories:

CORE : these are attempted (usually successfully by the vast majority of the class).

REMEDIAL : these are attempted by those pupils who have difficulty in completing the CORE. After completing these sheets successfully, the pupil attempts the CORE again.

EXTENSION : these are attempted by those pupils who cope well with the CORE. In these worksheets, greater demands are placed on the pupil, and additional skills are developed.

There are two main reasons for sending out this report:

1. to give you an indication of the performance of your child;
2. to highlight areas where that performance could be improved.

The categories given to your child are based on work carried out throughout the first term. This has been CONTINUOUSLY ASSESSED by the Class teacher.

Yours faithfully,

Principal Teacher of
Modern Studies.

Name of Pupil:	Subject:	Class:	Second
	MODERN STUDIES		Assessment

SECTION 1

Understanding of the concepts
of Conflict and Co-operation

	Understands the concept thoroughly
	Understands the concept well
	Shows an adequate grasp of the concept
	Slow to grasp concept

SECTION 2

Subject Skills:

(a) Enquiry;
    interpretation of information

	Completes core worksheets satisfactorily.
	Copes with core after revision
	Regularly completes extension sheets
	Completes extension sheets with imagination.

(b) Ability to express ideas in
    writing

	Expresses ideas fluently and clearly
	Usually expresses ideas clearly
	Sentence structure needs more care
	Has difficulty in using basic English

(c) Understanding of maps and
    diagrams

	Has no difficulty in understanding
	Has little difficulty in understanding
	Shows satisfactory understanding
	Finds it hard to cope

SECTION 3

Classroom behaviour

	Attentive, co-operative; works well without close supervision.
	Sometimes has lapses in concentration but usually attentive and co-operative.
	Finds it hard to work without close supervision
	Disruptive pupil

Further comment:

Signed: _____   Date: _____

    Class Teacher

Source: D. McGinty, M. McGlinchey and A. Kerr, St Columbo's High
         School, Clydebank.

*Figure 10.3 A profiled report to parents, showing the course objectives
             and assessment criteria*

Reports to Parents   185

In the NFER survey 58 per cent of pupils and 53 per cent of parents felt that the information in reports on 'O' level/CSE chances was inadequate. This was a major source of dissatisfaction.

Schools have genuine problems with predicting exact grades, and are therefore reluctant to do so. The difference between a B and a C may be the difference between acceptance and rejection at university or as a trainee. Yet the school's experience is still far more extensive and reliable than that of most parents and pupils (although the school has less insight into what makes each individual pupil 'tick'). A slight degree of over-optimism by the school in suggesting achievable goals is probably more healthy than depressing pupils' aspirations.

Another crucial developmental period is the transition from school to adult life, whether that means transition to further or higher education, to work, to youth training schemes or to unemployment. This again, is a period when the young person needs insights into his capabilities, apti-tudes, attainments and potential as a guide to decisions about his future. The great majority of pupils and parents (77 per cent of pupils and 79 per cent of parents in the NFER study) feel that reports provide inadequate information on their future chances on employment or further education. Reports, of course, at these crucial growth periods, are only a part of the process of decision-making, but have great significance to parents and students.

Parental and Student Involvement

In 'involvement reports' the emphasis may be on parental involvement or student involvement. Reports can be (and I believe should be) part of a strategy to actively encourage parents to become involved in their child's education. A personal letter from the tutor (Figure 10.4) accompanying the more formal report (Figure 10.5) is a friendly approach. This example is taken from exemplars drawn up by Vandyke Upper School to guide staff. Writing a personal letter to each set of parents is not an easy task even if you have, say, only twenty-five youngsters in your tutorial group. It is time-consuming and requires inter-personal skills. Exemplars are much more useful than a set of instructions from further up the hierarchy: they set the tone and guidelines for length, detail, balance and so on.

Increasingly schools are beginning to include parental reply slips. These often evoke little response unless some sort of personal rapport has been established. Sometimes this is purely an individual initiative. For example, a teacher of English in a large comprehensive school took the trouble to write long, detailed, sympathetic but critical reports. 'The content of Y's

Assessment: From Principles to Action

BEDFORDSHIRE EDUCATION SERVICE

Vandyke Upper School & Community College

Headmaster: Bernard Vaughan JP,BA

Dear Mr. and Mrs. B.,

It seems that D.... may be 'coming good' at the right time. Although there have been problems over one or two areas of his work, notably Geography and Home Economics, it seems that he is largely beginning to fulfil some of the potential which he clearly possesses.

Having said that, I believe I must emphasize two points which were neatly summed up by two phrases in the History report, namely, 'he must not think the battle is over', and, 'the rest is up to him'. Certainly D.... cannot afford to sit back, particularly with the mock exams approaching fast, and, in the next six months, he needs to work hard all the time and not just when the mood takes him. Secondly, it seems a bit silly to state the obvious, but when D.... eventually sits his exams in June there will be nobody to help him but himself! In some papers he will have to concentrate for two and a half hours at one time. Any fooling around in the exam room then would not only lead to disqualification from that particular exam at the time, but probably from all exams. So he must keep the sense of humour he possesses under control during exams, and allow it to flow freely at the proper time, and in the proper place (which does not include lessons!)

I have got on quite well with D.... and he certainly has a lively personality. Sometimes he pushes people too far and that is when he runs into problems. In order to improve his relationships with some people he needs to act a bit more passively and respond more quietly. However I am sure that, just as he has managed to improve in his work, with increased maturity he will find other aspects of life needing a different approach. I only hope that D.... does work hard in these last few vital months, that he doesn't have any more 'hiccups', and that he achieves the results of which he is capable.

Yours sincerely,

A Form Tutor

Vandyke Road, Leighton Buzzard, Bedfordshire LU7 8HS   Telephone (0525) 376838

Source: Rex Gibson, *Teacher–Parent Communication: one school and its practice* (Cambridge Institute of Education, 1980).

Figure 10.4   Letter from a form tutor, to accompany booklet of slips (some of which are shown in Figure 10.6)

Reports to Parents   *187*

Subject	Effort	Attainment	Name of Teacher
FRENCH	B	3	

I am pleased with D....'s standard of work and attitude; he now has more confidence in himself and can at times produce exactly the type of written French which is needed in the essay component of the examination. He must try to become more consistent and given a good term after Christmas and a successful oral examination D.... may well obtain a very good grade in CSE for which he will be entered.

Subject	Effort	Attainment	Name of Teacher
ENGLISH	C	2/3	

Although D....'s work has improved since the beginning of term, there is still a considerable amount that could be done to improve his chances. Too often in class he is tempted by his less attentive self to give only half his mind, and sometimes less, to the works we are studying. He is capable of getting 'O' Levels in both Language and Literature but he will have to produce more evidence of his ability if he is to do so.

'O' Level Language and Literature.

Subject	Effort	Attainment	Name of Teacher
P.E.	B		

D.... has worked hard in PE showing a genuine enthusiastic approach to lessons. It is pleasing to see an attitude towards listening and learning, and trying new sports.

Figure 10.5

	Subject	Effort	Attainment	Name of Teacher
	HOME ECON	C	2	

D.... is a cheerful and co-operative member of the group but he has a tendency to distract others and consequently himself. He has handed in three homeworks out of seven so far this term. When he settles down and thinks about his work he can work well; when he is being silly he is wasting valuable time. Practical work needs a great deal of care and effort, as also does the clearing up. He must do his own clearing up and not rely on others - charm won't get that past the Examiner in the practical exam! At present D.... is borderline 'O' Level. He must work very hard to achieve his potential.

	Subject	Effort	Attainment	Name of Teacher
	PHYSICS	B		

I think, I hope, D.... is at last getting to grips with Physics and making progress. There have been so many ups and downs that I can't be sure. He is still too easily sidetracked from his work by his bizarre sense of humour but I really do think he is getting somewhere at last. He will be entered for 'O' Level.

	Subject	Effort	Attainment	Name of Teacher
	HISTORY	A	2	

Because D.... does not work very well under examination conditions, I am entering him for the CSE papers in 1980. He has a _very_ good range of course work marks and providing he learns his exam material carefully he _could_ be within grasp of CSE Grade I. He must not however think the battle is over. I have been honest with him because I want him to realise what I believe he can do. The rest is up to him. A model student!

Source: Teacher-Parent Communication, op. cit., as Figure 10.4

written work', he wrote to the parents of one very able girl, 'is always interesting and very imaginative; she is particularly good at writing plays. Unfortunately she often gets so involved in her ideas that her handwriting and formal skills, like spelling and punctuation, go by the board.... I can't work out whether she really has difficulty spotting her own errors or whether she treats this exercise with the contempt she feels it deserves!' He then explains why formal skills are necessary. 'I am delighted with this report,' wrote Y's mother in response. 'It has given me more of an insight into Y's English work, which I would not have had with just a mark. I will also try to help Y correct her work more carefully as I would hate to see her marked low when she has ability.' (*Source*: D. Fairweather, North Kelvinside School, Glasgow).

It might be unreasonable to adopt, as a school policy, the writing of long, letter-style reports by individual subject teachers, but the school, as a matter of policy, can seek to create rapport by a variety of methods.

Research has demonstrated that parental support is a key factor in pupils' success. Some schools involve parents in assessment very directly. In these instances reports and records are closely linked. Reports are sent out, and then parents are consulted, to ensure that the school record has been seen by, and discussed with, the parents and (in the case of older pupils) the student. This allows extenuating circumstances to be noted, and factual errors and misunderstandings to be corrected. It also enables positive assessments to be entered into the record if they have been over-looked. Most important, this joint assessment greatly increases the chances of the young person, the home and the school working constructively together.

Increasingly in the secondary school years the young person him or her-self becomes the participant and audience. By the fifth or sixth years, students are often the recipients of reports, and make decisions arising from them. But the involvement can go further, and begin earlier. Here, for example, is a youngster's own self-assessment, which in this school, forms the first item on a report slip:

I don't think my work has got any better since my last report. This is really because most of the work I do is the writing up of a discussion for homework and I never really concentrate on homework. I often become very bored in the lessons because I think the discussions last too long and after a while of listening I tend to only half pay attention, then by the time I have got round to do the homework I only vaguely remember how to do it. I think it would be a good idea if we studied the different religions of different countries. I think this would be a bit more interesting than just working from the Bible all the time.

Source: Bosworth College, quoted by Derek Rowntree, *Assessing Students: How Shall We Know Them?* (London, Harper & Row, 1977).

In this, a comprehensive school, the teacher is able to comment not only on the pupil's performance, but on his perception of how he is doing, on goals and motivation. Nor does the process stop there. The comments are followed by a section headed 'Action'.

Student self-assessment is an approach which is open to individual teachers. It was discussed in some detail in the previous chapter (Chapter 9) as self-assessment is often used with profiles. Individual teachers have found that linking student self-assessment into the process of reporting strengthens the whole. For example, you can set, as homework, the task for each student of writing a 'report' on a folio of their ten best pieces of work, with suggestions for improvement. This can be followed up in class by small group discussions of the resulting 'reports' (children can be perceptive judges provided they see assessment as an aid to learning). Your own report slip may be the final part of the written process, to be followed by discussion with the parents and student.

Self-assessment is far more effective when adopted as a whole-school policy, often as a result of pressure from individual teachers who have used it successfully.

Some schools approach student involvement (and that often means self-assessment) rather differently. For example, many schools expect sixth-formers to assist in supplying the evidence upon which, at least in part, the head teacher will draw in writing a personal assessment for the student's UCCA form. 'Be truthful', one sixth-form college counsels, 'but don't be over-modest or negative. Present yourself in the best possible light. Remember, we've got to persuade universities that you deserve a place.' Useful advice. Many youngsters depreciate themselves and are very negative in their self-assessment (perhaps a reflection on negative messages they have received for years).

Similarly, some schools involve fifth- and sixth-year students' references that will accompany each individual into employment. The form from William Penn School shown in Figure 10.6 is part of the process of drawing up a reference – a process which involves the student from an early stage in his final year, but is not completed until he leaves. There can be a 'back-wash' if, for example, students know the format and understand how their achievements will be presented to future employers: they realise that the

Fig. 10.6 follows

William Penn School   Fifth-Year Testimonials

Shortly we shall be writing a Testimonial for you.
It will sum up what you have achieved in school.
You will have to show it as a reference when you go for a job.
The information on it will be used by the school to write confidential
references for employers, or to consider your entry into the Sixth Form
or Further Education. Read this sheet through and fill it in as fully and
as carefully as you can. The information you put on it will be used to
help in writing your testimonial. The more information you give the
better the testimonial we can write. When you have completed this
sheet, return it to your form teacher.

1. Write your full name with initials . . . .

2. Write your form.

3. Write the month and year that you started at William Penn: Month. . . .
   Year. . . . .

4. On the chart below write down your seven main subjects (English,
   Maths and 5 options) and the exams you are taking in them (CSE or
   GCE).
   If you are not taking an exam leave the space blank.

SUBJECT	EXAMINATION

5. If you did Community Work write down what you did . . . .

6. Sport. Write down any school or form teams you have played for, or
   any other recent sporting achievements, at Sports Day for example. . .
   . . . .
   . . . .

7. Write down any school activities you have recently taken part in, for
   example school clubs, plays, orchestra, work in the technical block in
   your own time:
   . . . .
   . . . .
   . . . .

8. Write down any posts or responsibility you have held in School, for
   example school council representative, form captain: . . . .
   . . . .

9. Write down any activities you take part in outside school, and give details of them, for example cadets, church clubs, youth clubs, sports clubs, evening classes: . . . .
. . . .
. . . .

10. Underline the things in the following sentences that most apply to you.
My attendance record is: Very good, good, average, not very good.
Punctuality at school, I am: never late, rarely late, sometimes late, often late.
In lessons I: always try my best, try quite hard, often try hard, find it difficult to get down to work at times, rarely work.
My behaviour at school is: always very good, good, quite good, average, not very good.

11. Tick any of the following sentences that you think apply to you.
I prefer practical work to academic work.
I prefer academic work to practical work.
My health is good.
My health is average.
I always get on well with my teachers.
I get on well with most of my teachers.
I get on well with other boys.
I am a hard worker.
I work well with other people.
I have found some school work difficult but have always done my very best.

12. What is your favourite subject in school? . . . .

13. What job would you like when you leave school? . . . .

14. Write down any other information that you think should be written on your testimonial: . . . .
. . . .
. . . .

Signed . . . .

Date . . . .

GIVE THIS SHEET TO YOUR FORM TEACHER

Source: Inner London Education Authority, *Record Keeping and Profiles: Guidance for Schools*, RS 837/82.

Figure 10.6
Part only of an extended dialogue with school-leavers, leading to the production of testimonials.

learning and developmental goals they set for themselves can (if they wish) become part of the assessment process, and that their own self-assessment can add positively to the school's understanding of their capabilities.

Function, Timing and Context

The timing of reports is of great importance for a number of reasons. First, for administrative reasons there is much to be said for staggering the reporting procedure, so that teachers are not overburdened. Writing a report ideally gives the opportunity for a calm and full assessment of the pupil's school life. Research shows (not surprisingly) that the more reports a teacher has to complete, the less time he spends on each report. In the NFER study it was shown that among teachers who had under thirty reports to complete, 68 per cent spent over five minutes per entry. In contrast, 71 per cent of teachers having over ninety reports to complete spent four minutes or less on each report; 37 per cent in fact spent two minutes or less. Inevitably, the quality of the teacher's judgements, and comments, are likely to suffer if he is overburdened and rushed. On average, teachers spend only six minutes on each report – a figure that hardly seems commensurate with the need to sum up perhaps a year's work (although the time spent actually with pen in hand and report slip on desk is far from representing the whole process).

There are strong arguments, therefore, for spreading the burden of reporting over the school year.

The second major argument for staggering reports is that reports, if they are seen as developmental or formative, need to be co-ordinated with the real dynamic of pupils' lives, seen as a continuous process through the school. A pattern is likely to emerge:

	TERM	SPECIAL FUNCTION
Year 1	Autumn – 2nd half	Description of response to new learning situation
	Summer – end	Full report
Year 2	Summer – early	Full report
Year 3	Spring – 1st half	Full report, specially angled to consideration of choice of options for fourth and fifth years
Year 4	Autumn – 2nd half	Description of responses to new course and grouping

Assessment: From Principles to Action

Year 5	Summer – 2nd half	Full report
	Spring – 1st half	Pre-examination considerations
	Summer	Leaving certificate

(and so on for Years 6 and 7)

(*Source*: Michael Marland, *Pastoral Care* (chapter on keeping in touch) (Heinemann, 1974.))

Another aspect of timing and context is the integration of reports with consultative parents' evenings. In the NFER study research showed that the majority of parents attended consultative parents' evenings. With the parents of first-year pupils and of sixth years, attendance was exceptionally high: in fewer than 10 per cent of schools did attendance fall below half of these parents, and in 59 per cent of schools attendance of first years' parents was in excess of 76 per cent, while 57 per cent of schools reported similar high attendance of sixth years' parents. Attendance drops somewhat in the intervening years, but even so, on average, in three schools out of ten more than half the parents attend.

Carefully planning, so that the reports precede consultative meetings, and meetings are well-arranged, pays off. A common complaint from parents about consultative evenings, often well-justified, is the long waiting periods and brief, inadequate, semi-public interviews. Better organisation, and possibly an appointments system, can reduce waiting times. Privacy is more difficult. In cases where it is essential, interviews are best conducted at another time. Adequate preparation for interviews, backed up by an agenda for action (a section on reports headed 'Action' is ideal) improves the quality of the discussion. A major problem for teachers is that neither in colleges of education, nor during in-service training, are they given training in interviewing skills. This is something which schools could and should remedy.

The non-attendance of some parents is a real problem, especially of those parents whose children are causing concern. The Cambridge Accountability Project in a useful and detailed discussion identified a number of reasons for non-attendance. These included the difficulties of shift workers and single-parent families; too great deference among some parents who were prepared to leave education to 'the experts' on the one hand, and cynicism among others who are put off by the one-way pattern of communication. A major problem exists for parents whose own school experience was bad and who feel inadequate compared to teachers (John Elliott *et al.*, *Accountability in School* (London: Grant McIntyre, 1981)).

In spite of all these problems, face-to-face interviews are often more effective than written communications, but are unproductive if there is no agenda, and an agenda is what a report provides.

Obviously reports often succeed (or fail) in making an effective impact in so far as they relate well, or poorly, to other home–school communications. Reports which have a context within good home–school communication involve parents better.

Fortunately home–school communications have begun to attract a good deal of attention. A disturbing finding is that most schools devote far more space to information about PE kit and school dinners and litter than they do to the curriculum and to assessment (which, apart from references to public examinations, barely gets a mention). It is illuminating to compare what your school sends out with that of other schools. There are numerous examples in J. Bastiani's *Written Communication between School and Home* (University of Nottingham School of Education, 1978); *The Book of the School*, edited by Graham Atherton for the Scottish Consumer Council (1982); and from the Advisory Centre on Education, *The School Prospectus Kit*, by Felicity Taylor (ACE, 1980). The most interesting, however, is Rex Gibson's *Teacher–Parent Communication: One School and its Practice* (Cambridge Institute of Education, 1980), which includes all the communications from a single school which has a clear educational philosophy on parental involvement, and very high standards.

Future Developments

We are in a period of rapid change. Well over half the schools in a recent survey had made changes to their reporting system within the last five years (NFER, 1983). The single-sheet report sheet was still widely used: 43 per cent of schools used these for first-year pupils, but only 33 per cent used them with sixth- and seventh-year students. However, there appears to be a swing towards slips, with 39 per cent of schools using these with first-year pupils, rising to 56 per cent with fifth and sixth years. A minority of schools bound their reports into books.

Interestingly, at the date of the study (1978–81) the profile was only just beginning to emerge. One of the authors of this report, Brian Goacher, was subsequently involved in the Schools Council project on *Profiled Reports for School Leavers*. Computer-assisted reporting (see Figure 10.1) appears to have been adopted by only one of the 740 schools which participated in the study. Only one or two used personal letters to parents as a regular form of reporting.

It is clear, however, that reporting formats are likely to change more rapidly in the last part of the century, for a number of reasons. Schools are becoming more responsive to the consumers of education. These include industry, further and higher education, parents and students themselves. Massive changes are taking place in education, and particularly in assessment. These are partly due to new understandings, and changes in educational philosophy and objectives. In some cases changes will be adopted simply to conform with contemporary fashion: a dangerous guide. Many of the new approaches offer considerable potential for useful development, but need to be intelligently introduced, within a carefully-thought-out policy, with a realistic understanding of their limitations. In concluding, therefore, I would like to consider some of the likely changes, and to suggest guidelines for change.

The Pattern of Change

Not all changes can be foreseen. But some trends are already obvious. For example, there are strong pressures towards parental involvement, self-assessment, profiling and computerised reports.

Parental involvement is likely to increase with the stronger emphasis on accountability. The cynic will observe that the need to attract parents at a time of falling rolls is causing schools to re-examine their reporting systems: good home–school communication is a strong selling-point. But schools are also aware that parental involvement fosters good learning. The inclusion of a section for parental response is already becoming important, even though it is often symbolic. Some teachers find the changing relationship with parents difficult to handle: there is less deference, and a greater emphasis on collaboration and co-operation in something more like an equal partnership. At the same time many parents are experiencing considerable difficulties with their teenage sons and daughters, and may be tense, confused or even hostile. Young people faced with many uncertainties, particularly about employment prospects, suffer a lack of motivation that is just as much a problem to parents as it is to teachers. More than ever, teachers need in-service training in interviewing and counselling.

Likewise, student self-assessment is likely to feature increasingly. New learning styles, based on the new technology, will necessitate more self-monitoring. The importance of involvement, of student self-assessment, has been a recurring theme in this book. It is nevertheless not easy to achieve, especially if the student fears that honest self-assessment will count against him, form part of a secret record. Some teachers also have anxieties, for it is difficult for students to assess learning without assessing, to some degree, teaching. This is something we as teachers will need to learn how to handle, for it is not easy.

Profiled reports, or profiled sections on report slips (see Figure 10.3), are likely to be widely introduced if profiles become common as leaving reports. Profiles have already been discussed in the previous chapter. The quality of profiled reports is extremely variable. They can offer a summary of curricular objectives (knowledge, experience, skills and understandings gained in a particular course) and this is a development I would welcome. Less welcome would be the substitution of 'little boxes' filled with ticks for the considered comments addressed to the individual pupil. Ticks are no substitute for what I have called 'quality' comments. The profiling of personal qualities such as 'self-knowledge' seem to me of doubtful validity.

The crucial factor in the adoption of profiles is, however, likely to be the new technology. A major objection to profiling is the tedium of manually filling out the form. All this will change as computer-assisted reporting packages are offered by educational publishers, and software houses, or mounted by the in-school computer expert.

Computers are already being used to reduce many of the tiresome chores associated with reporting. For example, a computer should be able to 'head up' reports (inserting the child's name, class, subject, etc.), and collate reports very efficiently. This will be widely welcomed.

Can computers be used to profile? Computers have an unfortunate initial tendency to reduce everything to numbers. This gives a spurious objectivity to the computerised report, but threatens to reduce assessment to a process in which numerical judgements are *de rigeur*. However, there are many aspects of the pupil's work which cannot be assessed thus (creativity, for example, or oral skills). Next, computerisation often reduces comments to a selection from a 'multiple choice'. These have a tendency to trivialise, and the tone is often one of robotic monotony (see Figure 10.1, p. 176). The proverbial 'garbage in garbage out' is all too true. Schools would be poorly advised to settle for either number-crunching or poor quality comment-options. Both approaches fail to exploit the computer's potential for creativity.

But the computer can greatly widen the possibilities in reporting. The computer-assisted report from Barrhead High School (Figure 10.7) is a pioneer attempt. On the screen the teacher is offered a 'menu' (Figure 10.8) and by pressing, say, three on the keyboard, option 3 ('READS FAIR AMOUNT. COULD EXTEND THE RANGE)' is selected. This is a standard procedure, but the text of each option is non-standard – you

                    ENGLISH   TEACHER : MRS

```
-----------------------------------------------------------------
I AREAS OF ASSESSMENT  I  COMMENTS                                I
I----------------------I------------------------------------------I
I READING              I  READS FAIR AMOUNT. COULD EXTEND THE RANGE I
I                      I  READS WELL. COMPREHENSION QUITE GOOD     I
I                      I  SLOW READER BUT CAREFUL                  I
I----------------------I------------------------------------------I
I WRITING              I  STORIES GOOD. PUNCTUATION NEEDS WORK     I
I                      I  HANDWRITING FAIR                         I
I                      I                                          I
I----------------------I------------------------------------------I
I SPEAKING             I  ANSWERS WELL AND SENSIBLY IN CLASS       I
I                      I  CO-OPERATES WELL IN GROUP DISCUSSION     I
I                      I  CONFIDENT AND FLUENT IN GROUP PLAYS      I
I----------------------I------------------------------------------I
I LISTENING            I  ATTENTION WANDERS AT TIMES               I
I                      I  PREFERS TALKING TO LISTENING             I
I                      I  NEEDS TO HAVE INSTRUCTIONS REPEATED      I
I----------------------I------------------------------------------I
I EFFORT               I  SATISFACTORY. AT TIMES NEED ENCOURAGEMENT I
I                      I  BY TEACHER. USUALLY RESPONDS WELL TO     I
I                      I  ENCOURAGEMENT                            I
I----------------------I------------------------------------------I
I ATTITUDE IN CLASS    I  WORKS WELL AND RELATES WELL TO OTHERS IN I
I                      I  CLASS                                   I
I                      I                                          I
I----------------------I------------------------------------------I
I BEHAVIOUR IN CLASS   I  BEHAVIOUR IN CLASS IS GOOD               I
I                      I                                          I
I                      I                                          I
I----------------------I------------------------------------------I
```

Source: Barrhead High School Report

Figure 10.7 A Pioneer computer-assisted profile
Each subject is given one page

could offer on the 'menu' the appropriate learning outcomes for your own course.

The potential is exciting, for the method allows departments to decide on what are the learning outcomes which are important and assessable, and then enables the individual teacher to use these options to create a profile of each pupil very rapidly. Notice how the teacher has the additional facility of writing in her or his own alternative comments if none of the options fit.

The Barrhead Report illustrates some of the teething problems we will experience with this kind of reporting. The printout (Figure 10.7) does not make very good sense. This is partly due to the clumsy syntax - a carry-over from the elliptical 'reportese' of traditional reports. 'Reportese' used to be necessary because the space for comments was so restricted. It is

BARRHEAD HIGH SCHOOL

1 ENGLISH

```
--------------------------------------------------------------------------------
:CODE: AREAS OF ASSESSMENT  : NO. : COMMENTS                                    :
:-----:---------------------:-----:-----------------------------------------------:
: A : READING                :  1 : READS WIDELY FROM LIBRARY                    :
:   :                        :    :                                              :
:   :                        :  2 : READS FAIR AMOUNT                            :
:   :                        :    :                                              :
:   :                        :  3 : READS FAIR AMOUNT. COULD EXTEND THE RANGE    :
:   :                        :    :                                              :
:   :                        :  4 : READS VERY LITTLE                            :
:   :                        :    :                                              :
:   :                        :  5 : FINDS READING DIFFICULT AND UNREWARDING      :
:   :                        :    :                                              :
:   :                        :  6 : READS COMICS ETC BUT NOT BOOKS               :
:   :                        :    :                                              :
:   :                        :  7 :                                              :
:   :                        :    :                                              :
:   :                        :  8 :                                              :
:   :                        :    :                                              :
:   :                        :  9 : READS CONFIDENTLY AND WITH UNDERSTANDING     :
:   :                        :    :                                              :
:   :                        : 10 : READS WELL. COMPREHENSION QUITE GOOD         :
:   :                        :    :                                              :
:   :                        : 11 : COMPREHENSION A LITTLE WEAK. NEEDS WORK      :
:   :                        :    :                                              :
:   :                        : 12 : READING NOT STRONG POINT - IS IMPROVING      :
:   :                        :    :                                              :
:   :                        : 13 : COMPREHENSION VERY WEAK                      :
:   :                        :    :                                              :
:   :                        : 14 :                                              :
:   :                        :    :                                              :
:   :                        : 15 :                                              :
:   :                        :    :                                              :
:   :                        : 16 : READS FLUENTLY AND WITH EXPRESSION           :
:   :                        :    :                                              :
:   :                        : 17 : READS VERY QUICKLY - RUSHES                  :
:   :                        :    :                                              :
:   :                        : 18 : SLOW READER BUT CAREFUL                      :
:   :                        :    :                                              :
:   :                        : 19 : HESITANT READER. NEW WORDS A PROBLEM         :
:   :                        :    :                                              :
:   :                        : 20 :                                              :
:   :                        :    :                                              :
--------------------------------------------------------------------------------
```

Source: Barrhead High School Report

Figure 10.8 A print out of screen 'menus' from which the teacher selects appropriate comments for the profile

not necessary on computer-assisted profiles, although clearly economy is commendable. The continued use of 'reportese' (with its subjectless sentences) may reflect an uncertainty about the audience. Is it the parent? If so, would it not be better to head the COMMENTS column:

COMMENTS: YOUR CHILD.....
READS A FAIR AMOUNT, BUT COULD EXTEND THE RANGE.

and so on. (With older pupils, the audience could well be the young person.) Then, too, there is a certain ambiguity:

READS FAIR AMOUNT. COULD EXTEND RANGE
READS WELL. COMPREHENSION QUITE GOOD
SLOW READER BUT CAREFUL

What is the parent (and child) to make of this? Yet a glance at the 'menu' (Figure 10.8) shows that the first comment is concerned with the child's reading for pleasure, the second with comprehension, the third with reading aloud. The comments need to be expanded slightly, and made more intelligible.

Some teachers would assert that the comments are meaningless unless the parents can see the whole range (the English comments alone cover over four pages). Yet the whole range of teacher comments are not public property in other systems, and it seems to me more important that the appropriate comment should reach the child.

Despite a few problems the Barrhead Report illustrates how a school can use very simple computer programs to mount a profile which reflects the school's curricular objectives. The report concludes with a note to pupils and parents (Figure 10.9).

Guidelines for Change

In the midst of these changes it might be wise to draw up guidelines, or a school policy. Particular attention should be paid to reports as communications, and communications with both overt and 'hidden' messages. Guidelines should specify:

* Layout and presentation: depressing 'hidden messages' are conveyed by lack of visual appeal, poor layout, the use of rubber-stamped signatures instead of handwritten ones and so on.
* Readability: many parents have considerable difficulties in reading reports, due to poor reprographics, blurred typing, inadequate space for comments and (the commonest complaint from parents) the teachers' illegible handwriting.
* Intelligibility: care should be taken to avoid the well-known pitfalls of

Figure 10.9 follows

PUPILS - YOUR REPORT........is designed to give you as much information as
                               possible about:-
                    How you are progressing in all subjects.
                    What your strong points are.
                    How much effort you are putting in.
                    How you are co-operating with others.
                            ....is made up of information gathered since you
                               started working as S.1. pupils
                            ....will let you see how you can improve the subjects
                               you are weak in
                            ....mentions things about you as a person, not just
                               as a pupil. How you behave towards others; how
                               hard you work; your attendance, punctuality etc.,
                               are all important.
                            ....gives your parents a chance to see what your
                               teachers think.

          REMEMBER, ASSESSMENT SHOULD HELP YOU TO LEARN MORE EFFECTIVELY
****

PARENTS - THIS REPORT.......is the first of its kind to be issued for first
                               year pupils in the High School and in the country.
                     ....is an attempt to give you:-
                        accurate information on your child based on
                        classwork, tests and observation.
                        an indication of particular strengths and
                        weaknesses
                        comments on attitude, behaviour, effort etc.
                     ....is about your child as an individual, not measured
                        against others but against himself or herself
                     ....does not contain marks, but relies on grades and
                        comments

****

                        WE WOULD WELCOME YOUR COMMENTS
                        ON THIS FIRST TRY AT A NEW REPORT
                        FORM. IF YOU HAVE TIME PERHAPS
                        YOU WOULD COMPLETE THE QUESTIONNAIRE
                        ON THE BACK PAGE AND RETURN IT TO
                        THE SCHOOL ALONG WITH THE SLIP TO
                        SHOW THAT YOU HAVE SEEN THIS REPORT.

****

Assessment: From Principles to Action

PARENTS' VIEWS

		YES	NO
1.	Does this report give you more information?		
2.	Are the comments helpful? a. Subject Skill comments b. Attitude/Effort/Behaviour comments		
3.	Are the grades meaningful?		
4.	Is the layout of the report clear and easily understood?		
5.	Are you able to form a satisfactory opinion about your child's progress?		
6.	Is it clear to you what your child's strengths and weaknesses are?		
7.	Is the language of the comments satisfactory?		

PLEASE COMMENT ON ANY OTHER ASPECT OF THE REPORT WHICH YOU FOUND
TO BE SATISFACTORY OR UNSATISFACTORY. YOU MIGHT WISH TO COMMENT
ON INDIVIDUAL SUBJECT REPORTS: AREAS WHICH HAVE BEEN MISSED: THE
REPORT IN GENERAL: ETC.

PLEASE SIGN AND RETURN THIS SLIP TO SHOW THAT YOU HAVE SEEN THE
REPORT.

_____Parent/Guardian.

Source: As Figures 10.7 and 10.8

*Figure 10.9   Concluding pages of the Barrhead High School computerised
profile report*

inscrutable marks or grades, obscure educational jargon, impenetrable
witticisms, and meaningless clichés.
* Interpersonal skills: reports are a way of paying attention to children as
individuals, and their parents as people. This can be nullified, sometimes quite unintentionally, by depersonalising comments. Compare,
for example, the dismissive tone of

'Smith, A. needs to pay more attention to handwriting'
with the more helpful

'Tony's handwriting is difficult to read because he rushes his home-work. He needs to pay more attention or his exam marks will suffer.'

* Creating a rapport with parents: the aptness, effectiveness and clarity of 'quality' written comments, and their ability to communicate with parents and pupils, should never be underestimated. The tone of comments is of the greatest importance. And what a pleasure, for example, to receive a report which begins:

'Dear Mr and Mrs Smith,

'We welcome this opportunity to send you this report on Thomas's progress. . . . '

'Increasingly', writes Rex Gibson in his introduction to his invaluable collection of home-school communications from one school, Vandyke Upper School and Community College in Leighton Buzzard:

communication between schools and parents has become a central issue in English education. The importance of good communications arises from three beliefs: first, that parents have a right to know what goes on in the schools that their children attend; second, that such knowledge makes for good relationships between parents and teachers; and third, that good communication will result in improvement in pupils' learning and attitudes.

[*Teacher-Parent Communication: One School and its Practice.* A collection of documents selected and introduced by Rex Gibson (Cambridge Institute of Education. 1980)] .

Assessment, Diagnosis, Plan

To be effective the school report should be based on a strategy: assessment, diagnosis and plan.

The topic of assessment has been extensively discussed throughout this book. Reports are a distillation of the whole assessment process. Parents have a right to share, through various home-school communications, some understanding of the curriculum and of assessment criteria, in order that they can understand the report on their son's or daughter's progress. This demands that the school should bring into the open its working practices and formulate a policy. The lack of such guidelines greatly hampers individual teachers throughout assessment and particularly in decisions they make at the time of reporting about how they should summarise their assessments and what are the priorities in their comments. Schools reviewing their reporting should hammer out, probably in a working party (which might include parents), a simple statement and working guidelines. The lack of such working guidelines on reports will greatly reduce the effectiveness of so much effort that, day after day, teachers give to assessment.

Diagnosis should accompany assessment. Diagnosis goes behind the assessment to identify potential which should be developed and problem areas which need attention. The teacher can begin diagnosis in his or her written comments on the report, and follow through initial diagnoses in discussion with the parents and, in some cases, the pupil.

The third (and often neglected) part of the strategy is to formulate an action plan. Reports are rightly viewed as motivators, and there is considerable evidence that they do motivate, but generally good intentions wither like rootless plants in stony ground. At the end of an effective reporting process a joint plan of action should have emerged. It will usually consist of a number of achievable learning objectives, often in the skills area (a plan to improve essay-writing skills, or note-taking, information retrieval, practical skills in science or home economics, for example). That is to say, the end-product of a good report should be a more effective learning strategy, strongly backed by informed and involved parents and understood by the student.

Conclusion

A discussion of reports crystallises many of the points that have been made in this book. We do well to remind ourselves that the main aim of assessment is to promote pupils' learning and development. So we need to be clear about aims and objectives, and share these with learners and their backers (parents). Assessment should be, as far as possible, a valid and reliable evaluation of how far these learning outcomes are being achieved. So the form of the assessment, and the way assessment is communicated, must be appropriate: fitness for purpose is a key concept. This implies that assessment is not just something which comes at the end of a course, but is an integral part of the whole educational process.

Education is a preparation for life. Adults only operate effectively if they have integrated within themselves a value system. Assessment is essentially about values and standards. Assessment is not just something done to pupils. It is a part of life: a strategy for setting objectives, diagnosing and solving problems, monitoring progress, achieving goals. Perhaps this seems far removed from the task of putting a mark at the end of that ink-stained exercise in a dog-eared notebook, or conveying to young Jimmy's parents your suggestions about how he could improve his spelling, but we should not undervalue the importance of this day-to-day work, and we need to recall that perhaps more important to young Jimmy than his recall of French verbs or his ability to solve differential equations is what he is absorbing from the assessment process itself.

We have tried in this book to bring together solid examples, drawn from existing good practice and newer approaches which are being successfully introduced. We have tried to avoid dogmatic adherence to particular methods, approaches and traditions. In assessment there are no instant solutions, no solutions which are universally applicable, no approaches or methods which cannot be improved. But there is undoubtedly considerable scope for improvement in our present practices. Moreover you can begin where you are now, whether you are at the beginning of a teaching career or you are a highly experienced teacher adjusting to new approaches; whether you are involved in a solo effort or are a member of a working party seeking to introduce a policy throughout the school which is flexible, robust, open to innovation but supportive and workable. Although developmental work on assessment makes considerable professional demands the results can be extremely rewarding.

References and Acknowledgements

The publishers and editors wish to thank the following authors, organisations and publishers for their kind permission to reproduce material from their work:

In Chapter 1

Sussex University - *Working Party Report on BA Degree Assessment*, unpublished, 1975.

In Chapter 2

Jones, Janet E. M. - *The Use Employers Make of Examination Results*, University of Reading School of Education, 1983.

In Chapter 3

Schools Council - *History 13-16 Project*, Holmes McDougall, 1976.
Schools Council - *Modular Course in Technology*, Oliver & Boyd, 1983.
National Working Party of the Scottish Central Committee on Modern Languages (convenor R. Johnstone) - *Tour de France*, Heinemann Educational Books, 1983.

In Chapter 4

Schools Council - *Geography 14-18* by Tolley, H. and Reynolds, J. B., Macmillan Educational, 1977.

In Chapter 5

Rowntree, Derek - *Assessing Students: How Shall We Know Them?*, Harper & Row, 1977.

Scottish Examination Board – *The Use of Multi-choice Techniques in the Testing and Interpretation of Language Skills in English*, SCEEB, 1975.

Scottish Examination Board – *Scottish Certificate of Education Higher Biology Paper 1*, SCEEB, 1974.

In Chapter 6

McKenzie, D. Castlebrae High School, Lothian – *Example of a Comparison of a Local Community with a Community in India*, unpublished, 1981.

McCartney, J., Jeyes, G. and Duncan K. – *Guidelines for Pupils on Writing a Report for the Modern Studies Special Study*, unpublished, 1982.

Schools Council – *Modular Course on Technology*, Oliver & Boyd, 1982.

Scottish Central Committee on Social Subjects and the Joint Scottish Committee on Environmental Studies – *Primary Secondary Liaison in Environmental Studies/Social Subjects*, Scottish Curriculum Development Centre, 1983.

In Chapter 7

National Working Party of the Scottish Central Committee on Modern Languages (convenor R. Johnstone) – *Tour de France*, Heinemann Educational Books, 1983.

Mitchell, A. C. *et al.* – *School Based Assessment and Reporting Using Microcomputers*, Glasgow College of Technology, 1982.

Further Education Curriculum Review and Development Unit – *Profiles*, FEU, 1982.

In Chapter 8

Jones, Janet E. M. – *The Use Employers Make of Examination Results*.

Schools Council – *Assessment and Testing in the Secondary School*, by Deale, N. Evans/Methuen, 1975.

Schools Council – *Research Study: 'O' level Examined*, by Wilmott, Alan S. and Hall C. G. W, Macmillan Educational, 1975.

Lewis, R. – *How to Write Essays*, National Extension College, 1976.

Jamieson, W. – *Higher Grade Modern Studies: Interpreting the Question*, Jordanhill College of Education (unpublished), 1980.

In Chapter 9

Scottish Council for Research in Education – *Pupils in Profile*, Hodder & Stoughton, 1977.

Elgin High School – *Example of Communication with Parents*, unpublished, 1980.

Dunbarton Working Party in Technical Education – *Example of a Profile*, unpublished, 1982.

Further Education Curriculum Review and Development Unit – *Profiles.*

Barrhead High School – *Example of a Computer-assisted Profile*, unpublished, 1981.

Careers Research and Advisory Centre, Cambridge – *Personal Assessment*, CRAC, 1971.

Bray, E. – *Example of Record of Personal Achievment*, Clydebank EEC Project, unpublished, 1982.

Blanchard, J. – 'English at Comberton College', in *Outcomes of Education*, Macmillan Educational, 1980.

Hopson, B. and Scally, M. – *Lifeskills Testing*, McGraw-Hill, 1981.

Pearce, B. *et al.* – *Trainee Centred Reviewing: Helping Trainees to Help Themselves*, MSC, 1981.

Evesham High School – *Example of a School Profile*, unpublished, 1979.

In Chapter 10

Goacher, B. and Reid, M. – *School Reports to Parents*, NFER/Nelson, 1983.

Marland, M. – *Pastoral Care*, Heinemann Educational, 1974.

McGinty, D., Docherty, E. and Kerr, A. – *Example of a Subject Department Profile*, St. Columba's High School, Clydebank, unpublished, 1983.

Vandyke Upper School – *Examples of Reports to Parents, in One School and its Practice*, by Rex Gibson, Cambridge Institute of Education, 1980.

North Kelvinside School, Glasgow – *An Example of a Personal Communication to Parents*, unpublished, 1979.

Rowntree, Derek – *Assessing Students: How Shall We Know Them?*

William Penn School, Dulwich – Example of Fifth-year Testimonial, in *Record Keeping and Profiles*, ILEA, 1982.

Barrhead High School – *Example of Computer-assisted Profile*.

Suggestions for Further Reading

In an area changing and developing as rapidly as assessment, it is difficult to recommend books that will not be superseded. We have limited this list, therefore, to a few key works which reflect in their variety and breadth some of the major issues in assessment, without losing touch with classroom realities.

Key Works

Works are listed in order of publication, as this illustrates interestingly recent trends.

Techniques and Problems of Assessment: a practical handbook for teachers, edited by H. G. Macintosh (London: Edward Arnold, 1974).

This authorative book, edited by the then Secretary of the Southern Regional Examinations Board for the Certificate of Secondary Education, is a sound and thorough exposition of good practice in the 1970s. Its approach is traditional and it assumes a norm-referenced framework for assessment. It is strong on techniques, and covers some of the major problems of assessment. It has a comprehensive bibliography.

Assessing Students: how shall we know them? by Derek Rowntree (London: Harper & Row. 1977).

Rowntree, a senior lecturer in The Open University's Institute of Educational Technology, considers what is the nature and purpose of assessment, and its side effects. He asks what should be assessed, how it should be assessed, how the assessments can be interpreted and how we can respond. It is a thought-provoking book, in the best traditions of The Open University.

Evaluation and the Teacher's Role, edited by Wynn Harlen. A Schools Council Research Study (London: Macmillan Education, 1978).

This book is concerned with how evaluation helps teachers take decisions about the organisation, methods and content of work in schools. Evaluation is, inevitably, based on assessment, and the early chapters in particular looks at evaluation (and assessment) of individual pupils, and the recording of their progress. It is a book which will appeal to teachers seeking to improve their professional skills and the quality of their pupils' learning. Drawing on the extensive experience of many Schools Council projects and studies, it offers a wide-ranging discussion which raises many interesting questions.

Outcomes of Education, edited by Tyrrell Burgess and Elizabeth Adams (London: Macmillan Education, 1980).

This book reflects the growing unease about the way standards are conceived and measured in our education system. The editors introduce and present twelve specially written essays which consider a range of possible alternatives to the traditional examination system, including profiles, records of personal achievement and other methods of assessing achievement. The writers are mostly practioners, writing about developments in which they were involved, under the editorship of Tyrrell Burgess (Reader in the Philosophy of Social Institutions at the North East London Polytechnic) and Elizabeth Adams, a former Inspector of Schools.

Keeping Track of Teaching, by Harry Black and Patricia Broadfoot (London: Routledge & Kegan Paul, 1982).

This book draws on and expands the concepts of profiling and of criterion-referenced assessment. It is a book for practising teachers interested in new approaches based not on 'selection' and 'quality control' but in helping to create a learning environment which is responsive to the needs, problems and potentials of each individual pupil.

Both authors are closely connected with the Scottish Council for Research in Education: Harry Black is a research officer, and Patricia Broadfoot was involved in the 'Pupils in Profile' Project, before becoming a lecturer in Education at Bristol University.

Further Reading

Readers will also find references to a number of other worthwhile books in different chapters of the present volume. *Details of authors and publisher are given* to enable readers to follow up particular points.

A particularly useful source of ideas on assessment are courses developed by the Schools Council, particularly those published in the 1970s and early 1980s. Titles will be known to subject specialists. In considering new course books it is worth checking the attention paid to assessment: even if you use course books as a resource not a determining factor, the criteria for assessment (or the lack of these) is a useful indication of the course objectives.

Index